POWER

Passive Option Writing Exceptional Return Strategy

Thomas J. Homer, JD, CFP®

authorHOUSE®

AuthorHouse™
1663 Liberty Drive
Bloomington, IN 47403
www.authorhouse.com
Phone: 1 (800) 839-8640

© *2019 Thomas J. Homer, JD, CFP®. All rights reserved.*

No part of this book may be reproduced, stored in a retrieval system, or transmitted by any means without the written permission of the author.

Published by AuthorHouse 02/12/2019

ISBN: 978-1-5462-7379-0 (sc)
ISBN: 978-1-5462-7377-6 (hc)
ISBN: 978-1-5462-7378-3 (e)

Library of Congress Control Number: 2018915198

Print information available on the last page.

Any people depicted in stock imagery provided by Getty Images are models, and such images are being used for illustrative purposes only. Certain stock imagery © Getty Images.

This book is printed on acid-free paper.

Because of the dynamic nature of the Internet, any web addresses or links contained in this book may have changed since publication and may no longer be valid. The views expressed in this work are solely those of the author and do not necessarily reflect the views of the publisher, and the publisher hereby disclaims any responsibility for them.

CONTENTS

Foreword vii

Chapter 1   Where's the Logic? 1

Chapter 2   Do You Have An Edge? 5

Chapter 3   Where's Your Alpha? 13

Chapter 4   Where Did It Go? 23

Chapter 5   Do You Have a Sell Strategy? 27

Chapter 6   Do You Know Your Options? 31

Chapter 7   Covered Calls 41

Chapter 8   Passive Option Writing Exceptional Returns 51

Chapter 9   The Greeks 61

Chapter 10 Market Timing is Dangerous 69

Chapter 11	Living the Wisdom of the Tao 75
Chapter 12	Sure Bets.. 79
Chapter 13	Know Your Margin.. 91
Chapter 14	Enhancing Returns – Reducing Risk 95
Chapter 15	End Game 101

FOREWORD

This book is written for both investment professionals as well as individuals seeking to supplement their income and personal wealth. Many people enjoy their chosen career even though it may not be particularly lucrative. In my case, I spent 36 years in public office. The work was always interesting and exciting to me. I loved being a prosecutor, legislator, and judge. I always knew that I could make more money as a lawyer, but was drawn to public affairs, where if you're an honest public servant as I was, the rewards are other than monetary. At the same time, I wanted to provide a comfortable lifestyle for my family and be able to send my three children to college. My wife was a stay-at-home mom who sacrificed her own career to raise the children. We chose to raise our family in an upscale suburb among other affluent families. With saving for college, vacations, dance lessons, sports, birthday parties and other activities, we often found that our budget was strained. I was expending a lot of negative energy worrying about financial matters and had to either find a way to increase our income or lower our standard of living.

Although a lawyer by profession, I was always interested in finance. Over time, I came to realize that there was a way that I could have my cake and eat it too using option strategies. The introduction of listed stock options in the 1970s - not the kind given by companies to their top-level employees - opened many new and exciting alternatives to traditional stock picking strategies. Initially, I started out writing covered calls. My first actual trade was in the early 1980s when I purchased 100 shares of IBM and sold one call. To my delight, the price of IBM increased ever so slightly, closing below my strike price. The call that I sold expired worthless and I still owned the stock, which had also paid a dividend and I got to keep that too. At this point I was hooked on the benefits of selling options. My purchase of IBM and simultaneous sell of a call option allowed me to make money three ways, namely the increase in price of the stock, the call premium and the dividend. The challenge was to select stocks that were more likely to increase in value than decline. A covered call position may lose money if the stock price declines by more than the premium. And the amount of gain is limited. If the stock price surpasses the strike price plus the call premium, the trader will regret having to sell the stock at a price below current value. Yet, he or she will have profited from the transaction. Intrigued by the concept of using options, I wondered if there was strategy that could over time outperform covered calls.

While still a sitting judge I studied for and passed the rigorous certified financial planner examination and earned the right to call myself a CFP. Upon my retirement from public service in my mid-50s, I became a financial advisor for Smith Barney which at the time was a division of Citibank. While there, I passed my examinations for series 7 (stocks and bonds), series 3 (futures and commodities) and received several financial planning certifications and distinctions. Later I worked as a part-time broker at a small Chicago brokerage firm while building my law practice.

Over the years, I have read nearly every options book that has been written. On family vacations, I could be found at the pool reading my latest book on investing with options instead of mystery novels like most sun bathers. While I learned something of value from each author, I realized after a time that none of the books provided a specific game plan on how to consistently make money. Many of them were filled with interesting and complex mathematical formulae and provided an analysis of the "Greeks" associated with options and option strategies. What I was looking for was something that would lead to consistent high returns, and I found the literature for the most part lacking. If I purchased a call on an underlying stock and that stock increased in value faster than the rate of decay of the option, I made money. Conversely, if I purchased a put option on stock that declined in value, I "might" profit. But how was I to figure out which stocks would go up and which would go down in value and when and how rapidly that would that occur? I studied the intricacies associated with butterflies, credit spreads, debit spreads, back spreads, time spreads, condors, and other cool sounding positions that could be constructed with options. But the success of these strategies was largely dependent upon predicting market direction and the accuracy of the forecast. I read how technical indicators and fundamental analysis can lead to profitable investing. Yet the stock market always seems to have a mind of its own and just when you thought you had figured out where it was going, it would offer surprises. It always seemed so easy analyzing yesterday's move based on today's information. Predicting tomorrow's or next week's or next year's market direction proved for me to be elusive. I was looking for an easy-to-read "how to" book, not one explaining esoteric theories.

Through trial and error, I eventually discovered a consistently profitable strategy and one that does not require constant monitoring or a significant amount of time. My Passive Option Writing Exceptional Return (POWER) Strategy is primarily for people who want to supplement their incomes on a part time basis. Whether a butcher, a baker, or a candlestick maker, you can keep your day job and make money on the side with little effort once you master the simple techniques outlined in this book. Using my POWER strategy, you will be able to earn a substantial supplemental income over the years without changing careers. It's not unlike being an operator of a casino or a life insurance company. By putting the odds on your side, you gain a built-in competive advantage. This is not a strategy for people looking to hit the jackpot or get rich quick. Selling options involves risk and is designed for conservative (yes, I said conservative) investors who are satisfied with gradual steady income. I have not been to Las Vegas in many years and do not like to gamble. The reason is quite simple. I don't like to lose money playing games of chance where I'm at a mathematical or statistical disadvantage. I prefer to be the House. POWER is intended to put you on the winning side of the table.

Most stock investors are long the market. Very few resort to short trading. Buy and hold strategies work great during prolonged bull markets like we experienced in the 90's. But as evidenced by the volatile markets during the first two decades of the 21st century, those who relied on such strategies were lucky to have broken even. Most actually lost money investing because of the psychological phenomenon discussed above that works against us. Utilizing the POWER strategy, we can avoid these pitfalls and consistently profit no matter the market direction. Having said that, there will be times when losses are incurred utilizing all trading strategies including for the writers of options. Losses can occur during periods of market volatility. The key to long-term success is to moderate positions, avoid being over leveraged, and be prepared to stand down (aka go to cash) during periods of extreme volatility such as occurred in 2008 and 2009. While being overleveraged can result in quick profits, being over leveraged on a losing bet can be devastating and career ending.

I hope you will find the lessons that follow to be as profitable as I have over the years. When you are ready to become a seller of options, remember to start out slowly and proceed with caution. Many years of profitable trading can be wiped out overnight for those who become too aggressive, overconfident, complacent, and especially when undercapitalized. Margin calls forcing you to close positions at a loss are killers. Remember the vast majority of amateur option traders come out on the short end when playing the options game with more experienced and professional traders. Don't allow yourself to become one of them. Educate yourself, start out slow and have a plan for all market contingencies. Happy trading!

CHAPTER ONE

Where's the Logic?

"A sane mind should not be guilty of a logical fallacy, yet there are very fine minds incapable of following mathematical demonstrations." Henri Poincare

While there are many books on options, few of the authors advocate selling naked options. Most authors are quick to point out that selling naked options involves "unlimited risk". Traders are urged to consider combining short and long option positions ("spreads") to take advantage of the trader's market outlook, while at the same time limiting risk. Other authors stress the risk-reward advantages of selling calls on long stock positions (covered calls). Many of the same authors who warn against selling naked options correctly point out that covered call writing is a more conservative strategy than owning stock outright. What you are seldom told is that a covered call position is the equivalent of a naked put (assuming adequate capitalization in your brokerage account)[1]. How then could a covered call be a conservative investment strategy when its

---

[1] A successful trader will have adequate capital in his or her brokerage account to avoid being forced out of a position by margin calls.

equivalent position, a short put, is risky? The authors usually don't explain. Each of the two strategies theoretically involves substantial risk. If the stock price goes to zero, a person would lose the amount paid to purchase the stock less the call premium collected. The holder of a short-put position would incur the exact same loss. While it is true that a covered call and its synthetic equivalent, a naked put, can result in a substantial loss if the stock rapidly declines in value, either strategy is less risky than simply owning the stock outright due to the premium collected.

If covered call writing is a conservative strategy and naked put writing is an equivalent strategy, why should we be encouraged to do the former and discouraged from the latter? Well we are told that the reason lies in leverage. In other words, you can generally sell more naked puts than purchase covered calls due to the different margin requirements imposed by your brokerage firm. While that may be true, having the ability to leverage more investment with your dollars is a good thing not a bad one at least so long as you do not overextend. It can also be less costly since you are paying only one commission when selling a put versus two separate commissions when establishing a covered call position. In addition, you are typically paid interest on the cash proceeds realized from the sale of the puts. Once you realize the illogic of the paradoxical claims that covered call writing is conservative whereas naked put writing is risky, you can begin to open your mind to the exciting new possibilities of the POWER strategy, a strategy that features selling equal numbers of puts and calls. If selling a naked put is the equivalent of a covered call position, is it possible that selling the same number of short calls and short puts with the same strike (a straddle) or with different strikes (a strangle) can not only be made less risky but potentially more profitable at the same time? You bet! Utilizing these strategies has enabled me to earn consistently high rates of returns over many years and achieve an alpha, which would be the envy of most money managers (more on alpha later).

One of my favorite subjects in college was a course in logic which has guided me throughout my career both as a lawyer, judge and financial advisor. Aristotle is credited with developing the concept of the syllogism from the Greek word *syllogismos* meaning "conclusion" or "inference".

Power

Syllogistic reasoning applies logic to arrive at a conclusion based on two or more propositions that are asserted or assumed to be true. A categorical syllogism is an argument consisting of two premises and a conclusion, in which there appear a total of exactly three categorical terms, each of which is used exactly twice. The most common example involves the following argument:

"All men are mortal (major premise). Socrates is a man (minor premise). Socrates is mortal (conclusion)." Socrates further proved the validity of the syllogism by dying in Athens in 399 B. C. at the age of 71. Applying logic to the main thesis of this book, I would make the following argument: "Covered call writing is less risky than owning stocks outright; a naked put is the equivalent of a covered call; naked put writing is less risky than owning stocks outright."

For the most part, experts agree with the major and minor premise of my syllogism. However, for reasons unclear to me, many of the same experts apparently disagree with my conclusion. Just like Socrates, I plan to prove to you the validity of my argument, albeit by less dramatic means. Where are Aristotle and Socrates when we need them?

Once you accept the proposition that selling naked puts is less risky than purchasing stock, you can with confidence reject the blanket admonitions warning you against the practice. Furthermore, you will discover that when you simultaneously sell puts and calls with the same strikes (straddle) or different strikes (strangle) with the same expiration, you extend the range of profitable expiration outcomes.

When you sell options, you are selling time premium. The price of an option is made up of two components, the intrinsic value plus time premium (option price = intrinsic value + time premium). The intrinsic value for an in-the-money call option is the difference between the stock price and the strike price, where stock price > strike price. For out-of-the money call options (i.e. where strike price > stock price), the option has no intrinsic value. In such instances, the entire premium represents time premium. Conversely, a put option has no intrinsic value if the stock price exceeds the strike price (stock price > strike price). No rationale investor would exercise the right to put (sell) a stock for less than it is worth nor to call (buy) a stock for more than it is worth. The price of an out-of-the money option, whether a call or put, is entirely made up of the time premium.

Time premium is greatest for at-the-money options. Since we are sellers of options, it only makes sense to capture as much time premium as possible. As we shall see, we best accomplish our objective by selling at-the-money (or near-the-money) puts and calls.

It has been my observation that most advocates of option writing, suggest selling far out-of-the money options since those options have the best chance of expiring worthless. While that may be true, by selling far out-of-the money options, the seller is leaving a lot of time premium on the table. I prefer to put that time premium in my pocket. The POWER strategy allows me to do just that.

CHAPTER TWO

Do You Have An Edge?

"May the odds be ever in your favor."

The Hunger Games

Most investment books on options offer strategies for profiting if you know which way the market is headed. If you are bullish on the market or a stock, you are presented with various ways of placing winning trades with options (the simplest involving the purchase of call options). Conversely, if you are bearish, you can profit from a short position (the simplest involving the purchase of put options). More complex option strategies, such as calendar spreads, butterflies, and condors, are offered to further take advantage of the decay in time premium and to limit losses. That's all fine and well but unfortunately, for most investors, market outlook is little more than guesswork. We may think that the market is over or undervalued or that a stock is poised to rally or fade. We may even have good reasons for those beliefs based on fundamentals or technical indicators. While there may well be some professional traders with the skill and foresight to predict what the market will do, most predictions are little more than educated guesses or hunches. I don't recall reading many predictions of the market implosions of 2000-01, 2003 or 2008-09. Unfortunately, for the average investor, predictions of market direction are amateurish and as likely to be wrong as right. At any given moment, the market and each stock in it are fairly priced with an equal number of investors believing it will move in either direction. Price itself is the actual indicator of where the equilibrium is on the supply-demand curve. So, if XYZ stock is selling for $100 share, an equal number of market participants expect the stock to rise in value as to decline. If there are rumors of a favorable event affecting the company's bottom line, such as FDA approval of a cancer treating drug, that news and the probability of it being accurate have been factored into the current price of the stock. Thus, you will hear traders talk about a stock being discounted for potential bad news and vice versa.

Moreover, by the time the average investor obtains relevant information, more sophisticated investors and professional money managers have already processed and acted upon it. Thus, at any given time, there is essentially an equal probability that a stock will increase or decrease in price, and that is generally true of options as well. I say "generally" because there are instances where supply-demand is not fully reflected in the price of an option resulting in an option being under or over-priced. Why is that? It is for the same reason that consumers willingly purchase insurance policies, or extended warranties on products, knowing that the insurer and not the consumer will likely profit from the transaction. We know the probability of our house burning to the ground or being struck by lightning is remote. However, what homeowner would sleep at night knowing their home was uninsured? We purchase insurance for the protection it affords us. We do the same with life and medical insurance. We aren't hoping to make a profit from the insurance. Rather, we hope that we don't. So, what if the insurance company is getting the better end of the bargain? It's worth it to us for the peace of mind. The same is true of extended warranties on expensive electronic products. We know when we purchase a new widescreen television or laptop computer at Best Buy that the three-year extended warranty is unlikely to be needed and that the $179 or so required to purchase the warranty is most likely not a good investment. Yet, we don't want to be the one consumer out of

100 whose product is defective. So, for our peace of mind we willingly shell out the money for the warranty.

The same is true for portfolio managers who purchase puts to hedge their bets and protect against a potential market implosion. It's much easier to justify the added expense of purchasing overpriced puts than to explain to investors significant losses due to the failure to utilize risk management procedures. Just like purchasing traditional insurance, portfolio insurance is a legitimate cost of doing business. And just as the insurance carriers and warranty companies are happy to profit from customers willing to pay for protection, so too are option writers like me.

We talked about the inflated price of puts. What about the calls? The purchaser of a call option is anticipating that the underlying stock will rise in value more rapidly than the call will lose time value. In other words, the investor is speculating. History is full of examples where speculators have paid exorbitant prices, thereby driving up the prices of a commodity or call option. Perhaps you've heard of tulip mania, a period in the seventeenth century during which prices for tulip bulbs in the Netherlands reached ridiculously high levels and then collapsed. The story of tulip mania is often used by educators to dramatize malfunctioning markets, imbalances in supply and demand, and irrational consumer behavior. So too there are market distortions resulting from speculation on call options. Perhaps there are rumors of a merger or acquisition, a good earnings report, or of an impending FDA approval for that cancer curing drug. Just as the price of puts is inflated by fear, the price of calls is inflated by the greed of speculators.

Moreover, as we will learn there is a relationship between puts and calls on any given stock. If the price of the puts is inflated due to an increase in the fear index (VIX) or the price of calls is inflated as a result of speculation, the corresponding increase in the premium will be reflected in both the calls and puts. This is due to the put-call parity relationship explained in Chapter Six.

As previously noted, the price of an option is comprised of two components, intrinsic value and time premium. Expressed mathematically, option price = intrinsic value + time premium. Intrinsic value is the in-the-money (ITM) portion of the option's price. Time premium is the amount of the option price that exceeds intrinsic value. For example, with XYZ Stock trading for $101.00 on June 1, the July 100 XYZ call may have a value of $3.00. The $3.00 call consists of $1.00 of intrinsic value plus $2.00 of time premium. Because out-of-the money (OTM) options have no intrinsic value, the entire price of the option consists of time premium. As an option goes deeper in-the-money, the time premium shrinks and may even eventually disappear, especially near expiration. At such times, the option price = intrinsic value. As option sellers, we are not interested in buying and selling stocks. That would require us to be either bullish or bearish on the stock. But we don't wish to forecast the direction of the price of the stock. Rather, we are sellers of time premium. We know with certainty that time marches on and that the expiration date for the options will eventually and inevitably arrive. At expiration, the time premium goes to zero. Yet, we sold the option at a time when the time premium was maximized. We will profit from selling options so long as the change in stock price does not exceed the amount of the premium collected at the time we sold the option. Time premium is greatest for strike prices that are at-the-money (ATM). Since we want to capture as much time premium as possible, we want to sell only those options that are trading at or near the current strike price. In-the-money options (ITM) have intrinsic value. However, we want to sell time premium, not intrinsic value. Call options that are in-the-money have intrinsic value and therefore a short call position is a directional trade similar to selling short the underlying stock. Conversely, selling in-the-money put options is a directional trade similar to buying stocks. As an option writer, we want to sell options whose price consists primarily of time premium. At the same time, we want to maximize the time premium. The best way to do that is to sell call options with a strike at or just above the current price of the underlying and put options with a strike that is at or just below the current price.

The time premium component of an option is also comprised of two components, the amount of time remaining to expiration and its implied volatility or market expectation of volatility. Because time premium is influenced by expectations of volatility, it is greatest for volatile stocks. While it may therefore seem logical that we would want to sell options only on the most volatile stocks, that may not lead to profits since there may be, and usually are good reasons for the outlook for volatile stock prices. That outlook is based upon historical fluctuations in stock prices as well as current expectations based on fear or greed factors. Being prudent investors, we want to be able to profit from unjustified fear or greed factors but not lose sight of the actual risks of price movements up or down based on historical price movements for the underlying stock. In short, we want to sell options where the implied volatility (IV) exceeds the historical volatility (HV). The difference between those two values can be plotted graphically. Utilizing OptionVue software, we can plot the statistical advantage enjoyed by sellers of at-the-money puts and calls. Historical volatility measures the past actual changes in the price of the underlying stock. Implied volatility measures the expected price changes in the future. With respect to the popular stock market indices, SPX, RUT and NDX, the implied volatility is consistently higher than the historical volatility. Why? Because investors and portfolio managers often need to purchase puts to hedge their long stock positions, while speculators are overpaying for calls in the hopes of hitting a homerun if the market explodes to the upside. These popular indices are used as proxies by hedgers and speculators. Thus, the buying activities of hedgers and speculators create an imbalance in the supply and demand of put and call prices, thereby driving up the costs beyond fair value.

The Chicago Board Options Exchange (CBOE) introduced a volatility index, known as VIX, in 1993. Initially VIX measured the implied volatility of the S&P 100 index (OEX) of at-the-money put and call options. Later, it was changed to the more popular S&P 500 (SPX), to gauge investor expectations of future volatility in the broader market. As an example, when the VIX is at 25, there is a consensus among option traders, based on their buying/selling activity, that the SPX has a 68.3% probability (i.e. one standard deviation) of trading within a range of 25% of its current level (higher or lower), over the next year. VIX values above 30 are generally associated with investor fear or uncertainty, while values below 20 suggest market complacency. For that reason, commentators frequently refer to the VIX as the "fear index".

Thomas J. Homer, JD, CFP®

The VIX rises when put option buying increases and declines when call buying activity picks up. Low VIX readings are believed by most technicians to be bearish, while high readings are bullish indicators. As you know by now, I don't place a lot of stock (no pun intended) in technical analysis or fundamental analysis for that matter. However, there is a high correlation between stock market activity and the VIX. It is an inverse relationship. When stock prices shoot up, most frequently the VIX goes down. When stock prices implode, the VIX can be expected to spike. The following table demonstrates the relationship of the VIX to price movements in the S&P 500 from 2000 to 2012.

Source: Bloomberg. Used with permission of Bloomberg Finance L.P.

VIX TO PRICE MOVEMENTS IN THE S&P 500 FROM 2000-2012

S&P 500 Up	VIX Index Down	Percent Opposite
1692	1390	82.15%
S&P 500 Down	**VIX Index UP**	**Percent Opposite**
1514	1187	78.40%

Source: Bloomberg. Used with permission of Bloomberg Finance L.P.

At the time of completion of this book in early 2019, the VIX is around 19, having retreated significantly after spiking on a closing basis of 36.07 on December 24, 2018. Such spikes in the VIX are infrequent. When they do occur, however, they present an opportunity for contrarian investors like me. Implied volatility tends to be mean reverting, meaning that the IV of options typically rises after it gets too low and falls after it gets too high. Spikes in IV that occur during market selloffs are generally followed by a rapid decline when markets stabilize. As a result, the opportune time to sell options is during market declines. For that reason, on days when the markets are selling off, you can usually find me selling straddles and strangles. I also use those opportunities to roll deep-in-the money calls forward. Near-term options are more sensitive to changes in the underlying stock than longer term options. As a result, the spread between near-term in-the-money calls and more distant at-the-money calls narrows during market sell-offs. During selloffs, I am able to roll call positions forward to a higher strike price paying a relatively small debit and occasionally with a credit. Eventually, in all but the most robust bull markets, the short call positions expire worthless.

During bear markets, there are times when even the boldest contrarian is well advised to take cover and wait for the storm to subside. The VIX reached a prodigious intra-day high of 89.53 on October 24, 2008 and closed on October 27, 2008 at a modern-day record of 80.06. There were good reasons in the Fall of 2008 for the VIX to reach these stratospheric levels. World financial markets were teetering on the brink of collapse. Bellwether banks such as Lehman Brothers and Washington Mutual failed, while the government rescued such stalwart financial institutions as Merrill Lynch, AIG, Freddie Mac, and Fannie Mae. Not many traders had the stomach to take a contrarian's role during that market upheaval, including me. It was a time that I determined was best spent awaiting some semblance of normalcy before getting back in the game. The following decade marked a period of relative market stability and steady upward movement, save a few temporary interruptions such as when Great Britain voted to exit the European Union in June 2016, commonly referred to as "Brexit".

In 2018, VIX fluctuated between 50.3 and 8.5, spending most of the time in the lower range of those parameters. Unlike 2008, the perceived adverse economic conditions in 2018 were much less structural, and while it took faith and some degree of courage to attempt to exploit the ensuing market volatility, the decision to do so has paid dividends. Anxiety increased substantially at year end in the wake of negative news. The trade war with China, the global economic slowdown, Brexit uncertainties, interest rate concerns, hawkish monetary policy, and dysfunctionality in Washington all converged to rattle investor confidence. It was also a mid-term election year. Interestingly, all 15 mid-term off-year presidential election years since 1962 have seen a year-over-year decline of at least 6.2% (the 2018 decline) in the S&P 500 Index. Yet corporate profits remained strong and unemployment was low. In short, there was no rational justification for the stock market to panic as it did in December 2018. During almost every negative news cycle, there is a fear that current events are uniquely detrimental to the long-term market outlook. While in such moments, confidence and optimism are in short supply, history has taught time and again that our economy is resilient, and that panic selling can result in an expensive overreaction by inexperienced traders and present enormous opportunity for more experienced and professional traders. See Chapter 10 for the causes and effects of emotional market behavior.

CHAPTER THREE

Where's Your Alpha?

"Nothing fancy Schmancy but she'll get you there Clancy."

Unknown Author

Perhaps you have been blessed with being a stock market guru. You know when the market is poised to rally or sell off and you are good at picking the next Google or Apple. Maybe IPOs are your thing or predicting mergers of companies or FDA approvals. If so, kudos to you. As for me, I know my limitations. I have too often over the years been surprised by market direction and have avoided providing clients with tips on the next new Apple. Frankly, after years of study and observation I think it's a crapshoot. It's kind of like the scene from *The Wolf of Wall Street* where Matthew McConaughey's character explains to young aspiring stockbroker Leonardo DiCaprio how no broker knows whether a stock is going to go up or down and all that matters is that someone is buying and someone else is selling.

Mark Hanna: "Nobody knows if a stock is going to go up, down, sideways or in circles. You know what a Fugazi is?"

Jordan Belfort: "Fugazi, it's a fake?"

Mark Hanna: "Fugazi, Fugazi. It's a wazy. It's a woozie. It's fairy dust."

During the three years I worked as a stockbroker, I was amazed at how generally worthless the sales meetings were. Usually, the meetings focused more on marketing and sales production than on the merits of individual stocks and for good reason. It was obvious that no one had any idea whether an individual stock was likely to go up or down in either the short or long term. It also came as no surprise that very few actively managed portfolios over time beat the S&P 500 index. Unfortunately, none of the managers, however bright and knowledgeable, has a crystal ball to accurately predict the direction of the market or of a stock on a consistent basis. Even the money managers who seemed adept at picking stocks with upside potential often lacked a "sell strategy". Thus, investors watched with excitement as their portfolios went up and with dismay as the portfolio went down, all the while wondering why the money manager rode the stock all the way back down. Why didn't he or she get out of the stock at or near the top? Many money managers fall in love with their stock picks and can't bring themselves to jump ship even when the stock underperforms. How many managers sold Enron or WorldCom near the top? Not many! (More on sell strategies in Chapter Five.).

In his bestselling book, *A Random Walk Down Wall Street*[2], Princeton Economics Professor Burton Malkiel contended that stock prices are random and argued that investors and money managers lack the ability to outperform market averages on a consistent basis. This theory of market randomness has since come to be known as the efficient-market hypothesis. Through detailed academic research, Malkiel demonstrates in a convincing manner the significant flaws in both fundamental and technical analysis, concluding that neither of these methods will beat the market averages over time.

---

[2] Malkiel, B. (2015) *A Random Walk Down Wallstreet: The Time-Tested Strategy for Successful Investing* (11th ed.). New York – London: W.W. Norton & Company,

The efficient-market hypothesis (EMH) holds that stock market efficiency results in current stock prices reflecting all relevant available market information. Per the EMH proponents, stocks trade at their fair value on stock exchanges, making it unrealistic for investors to outperform the overall market through informed stock selection or market timing techniques.

Not surprisingly, folks who make their living picking stocks for their clients, hotly dispute the efficient-market hypothesis. None other than famed investor, Warren Buffet, the "Oracle of Omaha", once gave a speech at his alma mater, Columbia University, refuting Markiel's theories. However, in a 2014 letter to shareholders of Berkshire Hathaway, Buffett revealed his instructions in his trust to the trustee for his wife's benefit: "My advice to the trustee could not be more simple: Put 10% of the cash in short-term government bonds and 90% in a very low-cost S&P 500 index fund. (I suggest Vanguard's.) I believe the trust's long-term results from this policy will be superior to those attained by most investors – whether pension funds, institutions or individuals – who employ high-fee managers."[3]

Apparently even Mr. Buffet has considerably more confidence in his own abilities than those of his fellow money managers. So, if you are not Warren Buffet, or a soothsayer, or in possession of insider information, you are going to need a statistical mathematical edge if you want to consistently profit from your investments. Casino operators and insurance companies would not exist without such an advantage. They do not "place bets"; they "take bets" placed by others, for a handsome premium of course. Then they spread that risk over many participants, bets, and time intervals. With the aid of actuaries, they can project profits to be derived from their statistical edge. They are unconcerned with each individual outcome - and are prepared to lose on some of their bets - to net the average yield on multiple transactions. It may not be as sexy or exciting as winning the lottery or hitting the jackpot but the majesty of the casinos and grandeur of the high-rise buildings in which insurance companies are located, not

---

[3] Letter to the Shareholders of Berkshire Hathaway Inc., February 28, 2014, Warren E. Buffet, Chairman of the Board

to mention their P&L statements, give testament to the success of their business models.

While I find much of Markiel's work in which he blows holes in both technical and fundamental analysis to be persuasive, I do not wish to spend time here supporting his theses or disparaging the erstwhile work of technicians and fundamentalists, many of whom, especially the fundamentalists, often hold impressive degrees and are well-educated. I can only tell you that most of the objective studies I've read support Markiel's premise that over time very few portfolio managers consistently outperform their benchmarks. I also agree with Markiel's preference for Exchange Traded Fund (ETF) investments rather than selection of specific stocks. However, Markiel's "time-tested strategy for successful investing" involves purchasing value stocks and adopting a classic "buy-and-hold" strategy.[4] This is little more than a directional investment strategy based on the premise that stocks generally rise over time.

Unfortunately, investors who bought and held during the first decade of the 21st century experienced some stressful and prolonged periods of disappointment.

2008-2009 "The Great Recession"

On October 9, 2007, the DJIA closed at its pre-recession all-time high of 14,164. In the next 17 months, the DJIA fell more than 50%. On Monday, September 15, 2008, Lehman Brothers declared bankruptcy and the DJIA plummeted 13% over the next month. By November 20, 2008, it fell to 7,552.29, a new low. The DJIA climbed back to 9,034.69 on January 2, 2009 before tumbling to 6,594.44 on March 5, 2009. Ultimately, the

---

[4] Markiel also advocates asset allocation and dollar-cost-average strategies, which I agree is a sensible strategy for buy and hold investors especially in 401ks and IRAs where short selling is prohibited. In his latest edition of *A Random Walk Down Wallstreet* (11th ed. 2015) Markiel appears to have abandoned his earlier recommendations for purchasing value stocks, i.e. those with low PEs.

market recovered but did not pass the 14,164 mark until March 5, 2013, nearly six years after its 2007 peak.

2001 Recession

The DJIA peaked on January 14, 2000, closing at 11,722.98, in large part due to the tech bubble. However, it started falling soon afterwards, hitting its first bottom of 9,796 on March 7. It languished before falling to 8,920.70 when the market reopened following 911. Threats of war drove the DJIA down further until October 9, 2002, when it closed at 7,286.27, a 37.8% decline from its peak. It was not until October 19, 2006 that the market closed above 12,000.

Before I started using my POWER strategy in real time several years ago, I ran multiple computerized simulations. Based on historical data what would have been the profits and losses from simultaneously selling puts and calls? The results were quite impressive. Being a cautious person by nature, I decided before proceeding to invest real money to present my results to my friend Jim Bittman, author of several books on options and senior instructor for The Options Institute at CBOE and at the Illinois Institute of Technology, where he teaches graduate level classes in the business school. Jim graciously arranged for me to meet with two professional traders at the CBOE for a lunch meeting. When I presented my concept of selling straddles and strangles, I was met with no small degree of polite skepticism. In the opinion of the traders, I had basically a 50-50 chance of profiting from each of my trades. When I tried to convince them that the odds of success were enhanced by the fact of the interdependent relationship between the puts in the calls, I could see I wasn't getting anywhere.

These professional traders pointed out that an equal number of market participants can be found on each side of my trades. Therefore, per these seasoned veterans, each participant has an equal probability of profits and losses. But wait I asked. When I sell both the put and the call on the same underlying stock having the same strike price and expiration date, aren't I assured of making a 100% profit on one side of the straddle, either the puts or the calls? In other words, aren't these dependent variables, rather than two independent bets? And therefore, aren't the odds greater than 50-50 that I am going to profit from the transaction? When I saw the glazed look in their eyes, I realized that perhaps I knew something about mathematics that these professional traders did not. Instead of being discouraged, I was emboldened by my discovery! One of my initial concerns in revealing the results of my study was that others would copy and thereby adversely affect the price of the options. After all, when there are more willing sellers than buyers, won't option prices become depressed I worried? But after meeting with these professional traders, I realized that if they did not appreciate the significance of my finding, there was little danger of copycat traders stealing my ideas. Not that I'm by any means the first person to realize the profit potential from selling options or even for that matter selling straddles on options.[5] However, I came to realize that the nearly universal aversion to selling options naked would continue to be a sufficient deterrent to copycats and that the space would not be filled with opportunists any time soon. Even now as I write this book, I do not believe that enough traders, professional or otherwise, will be likely to jump on the bandwagon. Thus, I am happy to go on making steady returns on my investments month after month and year after year in the quiet anonymity that I have so far enjoyed. At the same time, I wanted to tell my story if for no other reason than to explain my success.

You may also understandably ask how it makes sense to sell both the puts and calls on the same stock. Aren't you betting against yourself? To answer this question, think about a life insurance company who sells both life insurance and annuities. When a life insurance policy is sold, the insurance company is betting that the insured is going to live a long time. When an annuity is sold, the company is betting the opposite, that the annuitant is going to die prematurely. So, would the company sell both an insurance policy and an annuity to the same individual? You bet! The insurance company has built into its premiums profits based on predicted life expectancies. They are more than happy to take both sides of the

---

[5] See e.g. Schiller, J. (1998), *The 100% Return Options Trading Strategy*. Bridgewaters, NY: Windsor Books

bet by selling you both life insurance and an annuity each at a premium in excess of fair value. While they may indeed lose on one or the other of the bets, it is entirely possible if you live to your life expectancy that they will profit from both contracts. And if you die prematurely or live beyond expectations, the profitable contact – either the life insurance or the annuity - will more than offset the losing one. And in the meantime, the insurance company is investing all that cash and earning a handsome rate of return on its investments of the cash you paid to purchase both policies. Similarly, a casino operation will be happy to accept your same-size bets on black or red, odd or even, on the roulette will. While you and they will break even on most spins of the balls, those that land on zero and double zero will be their gain and your loss. Option sellers can emulate the profits generated by life insurance companies and casino operators, without the overhead.

If you needed to come up with a lot of money in a very short time, my strategy is not for you. Let's suppose it's Friday and you need to come up with $100,000 by Monday. Perhaps your uninsured spouse will die without an operation, or you are about to be caught for stealing that amount from your employer. It's a "do or die" situation. Let's say on Friday you have only $50,000 but need $100,000 by Monday. The best chance you have of doubling your money would be to head to Las Vegas and wager all $50,000 on a single game of chance, perhaps the roulette table. Put all $50,000 on red or black, odd or even, you choose. Your odds of winning on a single spin of the wheel are nearly 50-50 (47.37% due to the 0 and 00 on the table). You bet red, it comes up red, you go home with $100,000. However, there's a problem. You find out that there is a house limit of $200 on any one bet. The casino knows that its statistical edge derives from players making multiple small bets rather than one large bet. With multiple bets, the casino is going to earn its statistical edge of 2.63%. Consequently, if you plan to make 250 separate bets of $200 each, there is a strong possibility that you're going to lose around $1,315 (250 bets X $200 X 2.63%). Most casino patrons lose more than the house's statistical edge due to the emotional factors discussed in Chapter Ten.

If you were to flip a coin, there is a 50% chance of it landing on heads. If you flipped it 10 times, however, you may get 3 heads and 7 tails, or only 30% heads. However, if you flipped the coin 100 times, your odds of approaching a 50% success rate would increase. Perhaps you would get 47 heads and 53 tails, a success rate of 47%. If you flip the coin 1000 times, you are likely to see the gap narrow, perhaps 490 heads and 510 tails, a success rate of 49%. Eventually your success rate will approach 50%.

As an option seller, like the casino operator, you want to limit the amount of any one bet. Since you have a statistical edge, you will do best when you accept multiple small bets. Just as the casino sets betting limits to avoid huge losses, you have the ability to set your own trading position limits. Luckily, you can dictate the size of the bet. Unlike casinos you are accepting bets from unknown speculators, hedgers, and market makers. Your victims remain anonymous. There is no need for you to feel guilty. You're not even required to offer your victims a gamblers anonymous program option. Even though, like with casinos, you have a built-in advantage. There is no way will you be wiped out or crippled by a single bet. Having the odds on your side will lead to profits over a large sample size. There is no need to bet the house on a single bet.

Put and call options with the same strike and maturity are inversely correlated. When the puts increase in value, the calls usually decrease and vice versa. I say "usually" because spikes in volatility, either up or down, have a similar effect on both the puts and calls, making it possible for the price of both puts and calls to move in sync either up or down. Similarly, time decay has the same effect on both puts and calls, eroding the price of the options. Aside from the influences of volatility and time decay, calls track the movement of the underlying stock with puts moving inversely. The degree of movement is referred to as the delta of the position, discussed in Chapter Nine.

It has been estimated that at least 76.5% of all options expire worthless.[6] This percentage increases when considering at-the-money options, which

---

[6] Cordier, J. and Gross, M. (2015), *The Complete Guide to Option Selling*, McGraw-Hill.

are the only kind that I sell. When you sell both at-the-money puts and the calls on a stock with the same strike price (i.e. a straddle), or with different strike prices (i.e. a strangle), there is a chance that you will be able to retain the full amount of the premium you collected. That would occur if at expiration, the stock was trading at the strike price in the case of a straddle or between the two strikes in the case of a strangle. While you may not be so lucky to have the stock price remain unchanged, and thereby realize maximum return on the position, in the immortal words of Thomas Andrews who designed the Titanic "it is a mathematical certainty" that either the put or the call will expire worthless. Therefore, you will always win at least one side of your bet!

If the stock is trading above the strike at expiration, you will retain 100% of the put premium because the holder of the put would lose money if he chose to exercise his right to sell you the stock (assign) for less than its current value. Similarly, if the stock price is less than the strike price at expiration, the calls would expire worthless. The holder of the call would not be willing to purchase the stock (exercise his right to assignment) from you for more than it is worth. As for the side of the trade that is in the money at expiration, there is still the possibility that you will profit by the amount of premium minus the difference between the strike price and the current stock value. Only when that difference is a negative value will you suffer a loss on that side of the trade. But since you netted 100% on the other side, you have an additional cushion when evaluating the entire position. You can calculate your break-even point on the trade by the equation BE = strike price +/- the value of the two premiums collected.[7] For example, if you sold an at-the-money put and call on a stock with a strike price of 100 and earned $2 on each option, your break-even is $96 \leq X \leq 104$. In other words, if the stock price at expiration is greater than $96 and less than $104, the trade will be profitable. Because of the possibility that the stock price will fall outside this range, as it occasionally will, you want to limit the size of any one bet. Therein lies your statistical edge. Just like the casino, you want to establish "table limits" so that you will not be ruined by any one losing bet. By spreading your risk over several stocks options and expiration dates, established at different time intervals, you

---

[7] For a strangle, BE = strike of put - premium $\leq X \leq$ strike of call + premium

Thomas J. Homer, JD, CFP®

will be significantly increasing the probability of realizing your statistical edge over time. The same principle holds for life insurance companies. By basing premiums on actuarial projections based on gender, age, health considerations and other demographics, the insurer is essentially locking in its statistical edge. As the seller of several different short option positions, established at different times and with different expiration dates, you can do the same thing!

CHAPTER FOUR

Where Did It Go?

"Shame on us; for all we have done;

and all we ever were; just zeros and ones"

Zero Sum Lyrics by Nine Inch Nails

The age-old question is whether the stock market and options are a zero-sum game. During the seismic stock market sell off in 2008 and 2009, when the market lost half of its value, a client asked me an interesting question: "Where did all that money go?" She figured that if she had lost money someone else must have acquired it.

The answer is that the money never really existed, except on paper. The market capitalization of each stock is determined by multiplying the number of outstanding shares by the current market price. Market price is determined by what a willing and able purchaser would pay a willing seller at any given time. The "estimate" of that amount can be determined by looking at the current stock quotes. But until a sale occurs, the value is only theoretical. The value exists on the balance sheet of the owner of the stock. But until the owner places an order to sell the stock, the value is hypothetical. "If I decide to sell my shares, how much can I expect to receive?" The simple answer is the bid price if a listed security. If, however, at the moment the seller offers the stock, there are more sellers than buyers, the expected value isn't there. A market sell-off results when supply exceeds demand. At such times, market capitalization can change very rapidly. Money that never existed, except on paper, just disappears due to a change in expectations. Because of the constantly changing stock valuations, the buying and selling of stocks is not considered a zero-sum game.

The same is true of real estate. When the real estate market bubble burst in 2007 and 2008 brought on by the subprime mortgage crisis, a vast fortune in personal wealth of homeowners and real estate investors disappeared overnight. Where did the money go? A better question to ask is did the money ever exist in the first place? Until a home sells, its value can be estimated by tax assessors and appraisers. However, the assessments and appraisals are subject to sudden or gradual change. Only when a deal is consummated can we state with certainty what a property is worth. In the meantime, we deal with only projections or estimations of value, which is not real money. So, when we say that real estate prices dropped 50% or more, as they did in some places, money that never existed except on paper, was lost.

When a private company goes public, it sells stock in an initial public offering called an IPO. The offering price is determined by the issuing investment bank based on its projection of the market demand for the stock. Based on X number of shares, given the book value of the shares, what would a willing and able purchaser pay for the stock? The answer is whatever a willing and able buyer will pay to willing seller. May 18, 2012, was a big day for Facebook. The social media giant made its initial public offering on the New York Stock Exchange that day. The first day alone Facebook sold 421.2 million shares for $38, raising $16 billion in new capital for the company. Investors who were lucky enough to have connections with their brokers hoped for a big killing like those lucky few who purchased Google or Apple IPOs. After an initial decline in share price to around $20, Facebook took off and reached $182 by the summer of 2018 before closing down nearly 19% ($119.4B on July 26th (Black Thursday) after missing earnings and revenue expectations.[8] Nonetheless, both Mark Zuckerberg, the founder of Facebook, and other early large investors have gotten rich from the stock. But at whose expense? We won't know the answer to that question until the day if ever that Facebook goes out of business. If that were to happen the later purchasers of the stock would collectively realize losses in the amount of gains realized by Zuckerberg and the other early investors. On that day, if it ever comes, the ledger will be settled. But until that day, there need only be winners not losers. Not so with the holders of options which have a fixed lifespan.

For option traders, one trader's gain is another trader's loss. Unlike stocks, trading options is a zero-sum game, at least once the option has traded hands. For every trader who makes a $1, another trader loses a $1. For every seller of an option there is a buyer. The seller or buyer may be a hedger, a speculator, a market maker, or a clearing corporation. Consequently, saying that there are an equal number of winners and losers is not entirely an accurate statement. If you sell a call option you purchased at a lower price to someone netting you a profit, your buyer may also make money on the transaction if the underlying stock moves higher. Moreover, a hedger is not necessarily looking to make money on the option trade but rather wanting to transfer risk to another. So, it's not accurate to say that each trade results in a winner and a loser. However, option trading does not create any goods or services or add value to the underlying stock. In this respect, it is like a gambling casino. Money changes hands when people gamble but no new money is created. Only the Federal Reserve (and creators of digital money like bitcoin) can create money and only producers of goods and services create things of value. Option traders don't create money or anything else of value. Rather they enter a contest where they hope to profit from at the expense of someone else, except at least for the hedgers who willingly lose money in order to obtain protection from adverse price movements. The size of the pot is determined by the number of outstanding contracts at any given time, which in the case of options is

---

[8] Facebook stock has since recovered from declines suffered during 2018 in the wake of the Cambridge Analytica scandal, and other controversies involving Russian election meddling and violation of privacy issues.

referred to as the open interest. For every transaction, there is a buyer and a seller on opposite sides of the trade. When options expire, the amount expended by option buyers equals the amount taken in by option sellers, less commissions. Because there is a fixed day of reckoning, the expiration date, when the options settle, it is a zero-sum game. On that day, options which are in the money are worth their intrinsic value.

In a similar fashion, gambling is a zero-sum game. Gamblers enter the casino with the hope of walking out with more than they brought to play. The casino is hoping to relieve its customers of some of that cash. Unfortunately, either the gambler or the casino is going to be disappointed. Since no new money is being created, either the gambler is going be ahead or the casino operator. From the opulent appearance of the casinos, it is not hard to figure out who wins most often. An easier example is to consider a friendly poker game in your basement. Each of four players shows up with $250. At the end of the night there is only $1000 to divvy up, nothing more and nothing less.

Because gamblers and option traders are playing with a finite amount of money, they are playing a zero-sum game. And because option speculators are like the gamblers, they very often come out on the short end of the stick. Similarly, hedgers generally lose money on their option trades but they, unlike gamblers, are willing "losers". Like risk control managers, they are paying for protection. Together, the speculators and hedgers provide the option seller with desirable trading partners and opportunities to rake in profits on a consistent basis. We are more than happy to provide a cheap thrill to the speculators and protection to the hedgers at a price. Together the two groups make up our client base. Even if we never have a chance to meet them, we appreciate their patronage just the same.

CHAPTER FIVE

Do You Have a Sell Strategy?

"Study the past if you would define the future."

— Confucius

When I was with Smith Barney, they promoted the concept of separately managed accounts. Instead of owning mutual funds or individual stock positions, the client could "hire" a money manager who would create a separate stock account for the client. These separately managed accounts were more tax efficient than mutual funds and generally less risky than personal brokerage accounts since the money manager would be deciding what and when to buy and when to sell. The managers managed identical separate accounts for each client except for the total dollar amounts invested. So, if the manager likes IBM, he might purchase 20,000 shares and allocate a proportionate share to each of his accounts under management. A few of the managers had a stellar record at identifying stocks with upside potential. Some could boast of long periods of double digit returns and performances with a positive alpha. Alpha is the risk-adjusted percentage that a given portfolio or manager outperforms his or her benchmark, whether the S&P 500, the NASDAQ 100, the Russell 2000 small index stocks, the Wilshire 5000 total market index, or other investment styles. Clients were generally happy with the performances of these superstar managers, until they weren't that is. Many of the managers who led the pack during the 90s and early 2000s, got hammered in the 2003 recession and market sell off and again in 2008.

The problem for many of these managers was that although they knew what stocks to pick and when to pick them, they had no strategy for selling the same stocks, or any sell strategy at all. Often the managers seemed to fall in love with their picks and couldn't bear to unload them. If after a run up in share prices, the stock declined, that was a buying opportunity. The managers just had a hard time letting go of their stock picks or giving in when the stock fell into disfavor as almost always is the case at some point in time. If the stocks went up, the selection was confirmed. As stock prices declined, the manager would hold or buy more and wait for "favorable prices" or "a more opportune time" to sell.

I have found that one of the most beneficial attributes of trading options, whether a seller or buyer, is that there is an expiration date. That date, unless the option is exercised or closed out earlier requires the trader to take some action on a periodic basis even if only allowing the option to expire. There is also the possibility that the option will be exercised before expiration. Thus, there is much less danger in holding on to a position too long as compared to stock owners. At predesignated intervals – option expiration or early assignment – the option position will be closed. This forces the trader to take profits and losses at various intervals and avoid being wedded to his or her positions. Option expirations act as a buffer against having no sell strategy. In accounting terms, premiums received by option sellers represent "recognized" gains (or losses) with increased (or decreased) cash in their brokerage accounts, not just accounting notations based on "realized" gains (or losses), which have been earned but not yet collected. This may seem like an overly technical distinction, but there is value in holding actual cash, which can be reinvested as opposed to an expectation of cash payments at some time in the future based on the projected value of the security. As a wise person once said, "Cash is King"!

Traders must be cognizant of the IRS wash sale rules for non-qualified taxable accounts.[9] A wash sale occurs when the taxpayer sells a stock or security, and within 30 days before or after that date, the taxpayer acquires an identical stock or security.[10] Under the wash sale rule, an investor who realizes a loss upon a sale of stock or securities may not claim a deduction for the loss.[11] The wash sale rule has no applicability to transactions within qualified accounts such as IRAs. Moreover, the wash sale rules in taxable accounts have only a short-term effect on taxes. Since the cost basis of the new position is increased by the disallowed amount, the loss is simply carried forward. Detailed tax treatment of options is beyond the scope of this book. Investors are encouraged to seek the advice of a tax professional when filing their tax returns.

---

[9] Tax recognition for qualified accounts such as traditional IRAs and 401k accounts funded with pre-tax contributions occurs only when distributions are taken by the account holder. The distributions are taxable as ordinary income. ROTH IRA's funded with after-tax contributions accumulate earnings and make distributions free of federal and state income tax.

[10] IRS Code Sec. 1091

[11] However, the investor may use the amount of disallowed loss to increase the basis of the newly acquired stock or security and thereby realize the tax benefit of the loss when the new stock or security is sold.

CHAPTER SIX

Do You Know Your Options?

Option traders must first master some basics. My introduction to options came primarily from reading the excellent series of option books by Lawrence G. McMillan. His *Options as a Strategic Investment*[12] is the bible of the option industry and an excellent reference source. This book is concisely written with easy-to-understand mathematical explanations and examples of various option strategies. McMillan's weekly newsletter, *The Options Strategist,* is also an excellent publication. Another very capable author is James B. Bittman, whom I befriended in 2002, as I prepared to launch my second career as a Certified Financial Planner. Professor Bittman, a veteran floor trader at the CBOE, has authored several excellent options books including one of my favorites, *Trading Options as a Professional*[13]. He has an excellent way of simplifying complex concepts and providing useful advice for option traders.[14]

---

[12] McMillan, L.G. (2012). *Options as a Strategic Investment* (5th Ed.), New York, NY: New York Institute, A Prentice-Hall Company

[13] Bittman, James B. (2009). *Trading Options as a Profession*, Chicago, IL: McGraw Hill

[14] For more technical option books I recommend Hull, John (2017) *Options, Futures, & Other Derivatives*, (10th Ed.), Prentice-Hall, and Natenberg, S. (2015*), Option Volatility & Pricing*, (2nd Ed.) McGraw-Hill.

Following are some useful definitions and formulae:

Covered Call = Covered Write = Long Stock + Short Call = Short Put

Static Rate of Return = annualized percentage profit of a covered write, assuming the stock price is unchanged from the purchase price at option expiration, and the call expires unexercised. The static return calculation is made by dividing the income by the net investment and annualizing the result.

$$\text{Static Return} = \frac{\text{Income}}{\text{Investment}} = \frac{\text{premium} + \text{dividend}}{\text{stock price} - \text{premium}}$$

$$\text{Annualized rate of return} = \text{Static Return} \times \frac{365}{\text{No. Days in Trade}}$$

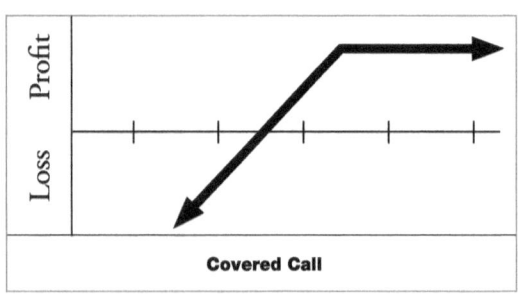

Covered Call

Equivalencies (Synthetics):

    Long Stock = Long Call + Short Put
    Short Stock = Long Put + Short Call
    Short Put = Long Stock + Short Call
    Short Call = Short Stock + Short Put
    Long Call = Long Stock + Long Put
    Long Put = Short Stock + Short Call

Long Straddle:

Long Call + Long Put with same strike and expiration

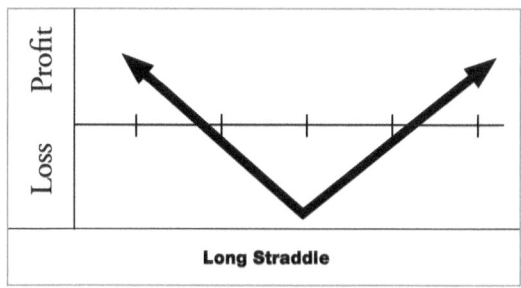

Short Straddle:

Short Call + Short Put with same strike and expiration

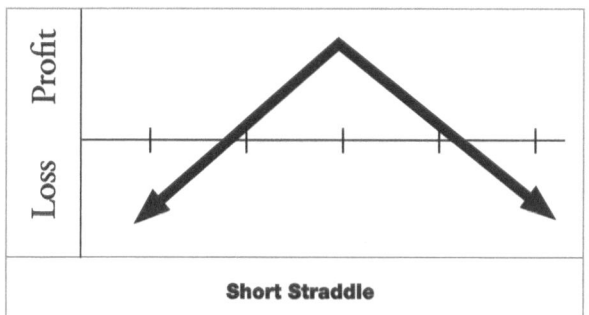

Long Strangle:

Long Call + Long Put with same expiration but different strikes

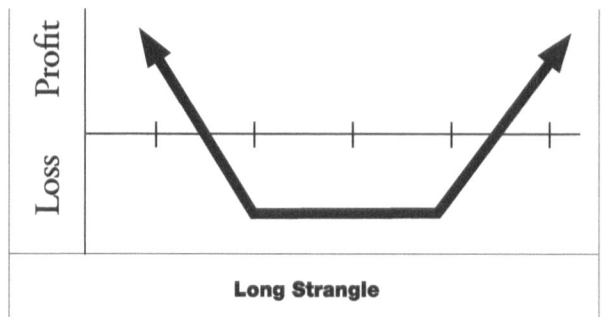

Long Strangle

Short Strangle:

> Short Call + Short Put with same expiration but different strikes

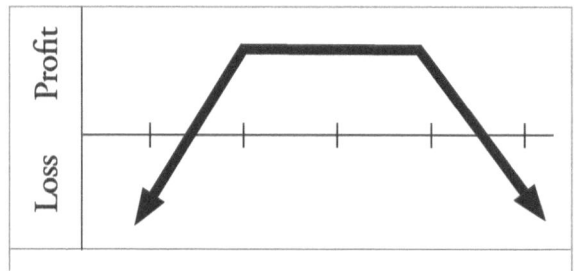

Breakeven Points - There are upside and downside break-even points for the short straddle and strangle positions:

Short Straddle:

- Breakeven Points = Strike Price ± Net Premium Received

Short Strangle:

- Upper Breakeven Point = Strike Price of Short Call + Net Premium Received

- Lower Breakeven Point = Strike Price of Short Put - Net Premium Received

For example, consider the following short strangle:

XYZ = 100
Mar short 105 call = 2
Mar short 95 put = 2
Upside break even at March expiration = 105 + 4 = 109
Downside break even at March expiration = 95 – 4 = 91

The position will profit with XYZ trading below 109 and above 91 at expiration and lose. if XYZ is trading above or below the breakeven points.

Conversions and Reversals:

In a conversion, a trader buys the stock while selling the synthetic option position in order to capture possible inefficiencies in pricing. For example, the trader purchases 100 shares of XYZ and at the same time sells a call and purchases a put at the strike price nearest to the market price of the stock. Conversely, in a reversal the trader sells short 100 shares of XYZ while buying back synthetically by buying a call and selling a put. Both conversions and reversals are used by arbitragers and market makers in order to profit from mispricing or manage risk. In actively traded markets, the pricing discrepancies disappear very rapidly as these trades are implemented by professional traders with the aid of high speed computers and using advanced software. As a result, it is impractical for passive investors to compete in this arena. In addition to being profitable for the professional arbitragers, the trading activity has the effect of removing market inefficiencies in which calls are mispriced with respect to puts or in which the options are mispriced with respect to the underlying stock.

Generally, in order for the average investor to profit from stock and option transactions, the investor must correctly predict the market direction of the stock. Such decisions can be based upon fundamental or technical analysis in which the investor is able to outsmart the investor who takes the opposite side of the trades. Keep in mind that there are professional traders who make fortunes relying upon the latest detailed information regarding the company or advanced computer technology that is unavailable to the small investor. The profits generated by professional traders come most often from the pockets of less sophisticated and experienced investors like you and me. In order for the passive investor to consistently make profits from trading stocks and options, he needs an advantage based upon mathematical principles.

Many brokerage firms that specialize in option trading offer online tools to calculate the delta of your positions. Advocates of pure delta neutral strategies would adjust their positions on a daily basis to make sure that they remain delta neutral. Due to normal market volatility, I admit that I am not a purest when it comes to maintaining such strict adherence. To do so, would require you to constantly chase your tail. While my newly initiated positions, selling equal numbers of at-the-money puts and calls, are by definition delta neutral, I anticipate that they will fluctuate between minus and positive deltas in the normal course of market fluctuations. However, I do try to maintain an equal number of short puts and calls. Occasionally, I am assigned the underlying securities due to exercise by a counterparty to the trade. For example, if I am short 10 puts on XYZ which are deep-in-the money, it is very possible that a counter party will exercise his or her right to put (assign) 1500 shares of the underlying stock to me at the strike price before expiration. Similarly, if I am short 15 calls which are deep-in-the-money, I may be assigned and find that I am now short 1500 shares of the stock. In attempting to keep in balance the number of short puts and calls, I can easily calculate the total puts and calls by recognizing that a 1500- long position in the stock is the equivalent of being long 15 calls and short 15 puts. Conversely, a 500-short position is the equivalent of being short 5 calls and long 5 puts. If my goal is to have an equal number of short puts and calls, I can simply buy or sell a sufficient number of puts and calls to accomplish that objective. For example, after being assigned, let's suppose I have the following positions in XYZ stock:

> Long 1500 shares of XYZ (15 long calls + 15 short puts)
> Short 500 shares of XYZ (5 short calls + 5 long puts)
> Short 30 calls of XYZ
> Short 15 puts of XYZ

My net position is:

Calls = 15 − 5 - 30 = - 20 (short 20 calls)
Puts = -15 + 5 - 15 = - 25 (short 25 puts)

To achieve balance, I will need to sell 5 new ATM calls or buy back (close) 5 puts. Will that make me delta neutral? Not necessarily. My delta position will depend upon how close my puts and calls are to being in the money. But I will have accomplished my objective of staying in balance so that when the market returns to its original levels, my positions will become delta neutral. Experience has shown that markets tend to fluctuate around a mean. Rather than chase the market, I prefer to let it come back to me. If it continues to trend, my newly established at-the-money positions will frequently allow me to maintain overall profitable positions.

Put-Call Parity

Intuitively, you might expect that the price of a call and put would be the same if the stock was trading at the strike price. If so, you may be surprised to note that there is a slight variance between the two prices. Why is that? It is because of interest rates, dividends and the time value of money. The owner of a call has the right but not the obligation to purchase the stock. As a result, he is saving money by not having to expend the funds required to purchase the stock at the present time. Because of the ability of a trader to create a call or put synthetically with the use of the other, coupled with effect of interest rates and dividends, there is a mathematical relationship between puts and calls. Similarly, as the price of a call increases due to changes in implied volatility, so too will put prices. This relationship is known as put-call parity. During periods of increasing volatility, both puts and calls become more expensive, creating the optimal opportunity for the option seller. That is why we prefer to wait for market sell-offs to establish our short option positions. We want to sell options during periods of high volatility. The relationship between puts and calls allows for the creation of one from combinations of the other.

Put-call parity is believed to have been first recognized by Professor Hans Stoll in 1969.[15]

$$C + X/(1+r)^t = S_0 + P$$

C = Call Premium   r = Interest Rate
P = Put Premium   t = Time
X = Strike Price S_0 = Initial Price of Stock

The good news is that you don't have to be a Penn Professor to appreciate the significance of this formula. It is only important for us to understand that the prices of puts and calls are related in such way that one can be expressed in terms of the other.

Put-Call Parity Formulae:

put price = call price − stock price + strike price

call price = stock price + put price − strike price

stock price = call price − put price + strike price

call price − put price = stock price − stock price

So, for XYZ stock with 60 days to expiration:

Stock Price = $65,

Call Price = $8, and

Strike Price = $60

---

[15] Stoll, Hans, Associate Professor of Finance, University of Pennsylvania, "The Relationship between Put and Call Option Prices," *The Journal of Finance* (1969).

You would expect the Put Price = $3 ($8 - $65 + $60)

Were it not for put-call parity, the arbitragers would be able to consistently make profitable, riskless trades until put-call parity was restored buying the put and selling the call or vice versa at favorable price disparities. As a result, when the IV increases in puts it similarly increases in calls (and vice versa for decreases in IV). Therefore, for example, when a trader is considering whether to establish a covered write position on a given call (i.e, buying the stock and simultaneously selling a call) vs writing a naked put on the stock (the synthetic equivalent), he need not favor one position over the other based on IV. While there may be momentary imbalances between the two positions (covered call vs. naked put), arbitrageurs using high-powered computers and sophisticated software will quickly capitalize on such market inefficacies by purchasing the cheaper of the two positions and simultaneously selling the more expensive one. The consequence of such market activity will be to bring the two positions back into parity. While the early days of listed options sometimes presented arbitrage opportunities to traders due to market inefficiencies, only those with the most advanced technologies are able to profit from arbitrage opportunities in today's markets.

CHAPTER SEVEN

Covered Calls

"Time, time, time is on my side, yes it is"

-The Rolling Stones

As previously discussed a naked put and a covered call have the same profit loss profile. Said another way, a naked put is the synthetic equivalent of a long stock and short call position. The position is profitable if at expiration the price of the stock equals or exceeds the purchase price of the stock minus the premium collected. Break even = Purchase price of stock – premium of call. While I prefer to be delta neutral by selling straddles and strangles, this strategy is not available in tax-qualified accounts such as Traditional or ROTH IRA accounts. That is because such accounts cannot be traded on margin. IRAs must be held in cash accounts rather than margin accounts. Because naked option writing must always be done in a margin account, the strategy is not allowed in IRA accounts. This may seem a bit illogical, since a short put (which is disallowed) is the equivalent of a covered call position (which is allowed).

Thomas J. Homer, JD, CFP®

Trifecta

Nevertheless, buy-write strategies can be very profitable in side-ways and up trending markets. The investor who purchases stock and at the same time writes slightly below at-the-money calls stands to profit three ways. If the stock closes at or above the strike price, the investor will earn the difference between the strike price and the purchase price of the stock. In addition, he will be able to retain the premium received for the call. Finally, he will earn any dividends paid on the stock prior to assignment.

The maximum gain then can be represented as follows: strike price – stock purchase price + premium + dividends if any.

The maximum loss is equal to: Stock purchase price – premium received

Following is the profit-loss graph for a covered call position (long stock + short call).

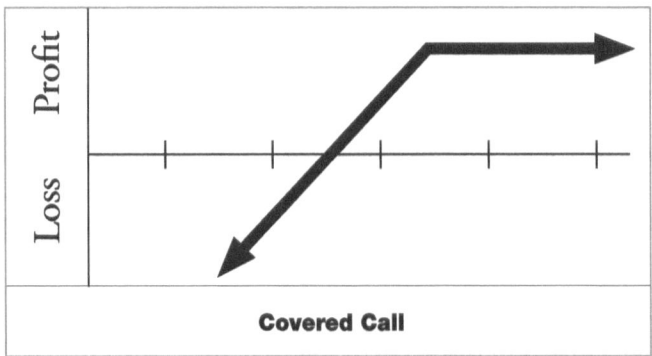

Note that the maximum loss for a covered call position is less than for an uncovered long position in the stock. Both positions carry risk. However, the risk of a covered call position is at least partially offset by the premium collected. Using a logic syllogism, a covered call position is less risky than a long position in the stock; a short put is the equivalent of a covered call; therefore, a short-put position is less risky than a long stock position. Furthermore, a naked straddle consisting of both a naked put and naked call, is generally less risky than a naked put position. Putting all of this together, this analysis should debunk statements made by many option gurus to the effect that naked option selling should be avoided at all costs due to "limited profit potential and unlimited risk".

By the way, you may be wondering about the difference between a covered call and a buy-write position since the two terms are often used interchangeably. A buy-write is often used to describe a transaction where the investor buys the stock and writes (sells) the option at the same time, whereas a covered call position can refer to the situation where the investor sells an option against stock he already owns. The result, however, is the same under both scenarios. Once established, you have a covered call position, which is the equivalent of a naked put.

A covered call or buy-write strategy works very well during periods of up-trending or sideways markets and in addition provides some measure of protection in down markets. I have very successfully employed a buy-write strategy in my own and my clients' IRA accounts. Due to the beneficial tax treatment of qualified (IRA) accounts, which provides deferred taxation for Traditional IRAs and tax-free accumulations for ROTH IRA accounts, the strategy is ideally suited for these types of accounts. Moreover, because tax recognition is postponed for traditional IRAs until the account owner takes distributions and completely ignored for transactions in ROTH IRAs, these types of accounts are ideally suited for the covered call (buy-write) strategies.

Even more importantly, the returns for covered call (buy-write) strategies, have been shown during most periods to equal or surpass the S&P 500 index and with less volatility. Several closed-end mutual funds offer securities which employ buy-write strategies. However, you can emulate those securities without paying the management fees associated with the funds.

With the covered call (buy-write) strategy you will beat the S&P 500 during periods of declining and sideways markets as well as during periods of moderate growth. The only time that the S&P will outperform is during periods of prolonged market rallies. And even during the rallies, you will be making the maximum return on your covered call (buy-write) positions.

To determine the merit of covered call strategies, the Chicago Board Options Exchange commissioned a study in 2002 to compare buy-write strategies with passive investments in the S&P 500 index. The buy-write Index (BXM) was developed by the CBOE in cooperation with Standard & Poor's to track the performance of a hypothetical buy-write strategy on the S&P 500 Index.

To assist in the development of the BXM Index, the CBOE commissioned Professor Robert Whaley to compile and analyze relevant data from June 1988 through December 2001. Data on daily BXM prices now are available from June 30, 1986, to the present time. The BXM is a passive total return index based on (1) buying an S&P 500 stock index portfolio, and (2) "writing" (or selling) the near-term S&P 500 Index (SPX^{SM}) "covered" call option, generally on the third Friday of each month. The SPX call written will have about one month remaining to expiration, with an exercise price just above the prevailing index level (i.e., slightly out of the money). The SPX call is held until expiration and cash settled, at which time a new one-month, near-the-money call is written. Please visit the BXM FAQ for more information about the construction of the index.

A performance review of results of the BXM for the period June 1986 through January 2012 commissioned by the CBOE[16] came up with the following summary of results for the BXM Index:

- Outperformed the S&P 500 Index in periods of static and falling markets.[17]

- Similar returns as S&P 500 with less volatility

---

[16] Hewitt Ennisknupp, an Aon Company, *The CBOE S&P 500 BuyWrite Index (BXM)* – A Review of Performance

[17] Tends to underperform the S&P 500 Index during periods of sharply rising markets.

- Return in excess of all other comparative indices

- Standard deviation lower than all other equity and commodity indices

- Standard deviation lower than the 30-year Treasury Index

- Sharpe ratio that was superior to that of other equity and commodity indices evaluated

- Potential solution for investors concerned about reducing portfolio volatility

Covered call strategies can be employed with any underlying security on which there are listed options. I prefer to implement the strategy using popular broad-based index ETFs such as SPY (based on the S&P 500 Index), QQQ (based on the Nasdaq 100 Index), IWM (based on the Russell 2000 Index), and sometimes DIA (based on the Dow 30 Index), although the first three are my favorites due to their high-volume trading activity and narrow bid-offer spreads. I generally enter new 3-month at-the-money (actually slightly above the ATM) positions upon expiration of the near-term options. By rolling the positions forward in this manner, using three or four different ETFs, provides the well-known benefits of diversification, laddering and dollar cost averaging to the investment mix.

In strong up-trending markets, I will often roll near-term in-the-money options diagonally (meaning up and out). This technique is particularly inviting during periods of market retracement since short-term options are more sensitive to price changes in the underlying. Frequently, the rolled-out position can be implemented for little or no cost due to swapping Theta (time premium). In other words, you are able to sell time premium to offset the higher price of calls with a higher strike price. For example, let's say on June 21 you established a covered call position in 1000 shares of XYZ stock trading at $100 per share and sold 10 September 105 calls for $2. Now it's August, the price of XYZ has increased to $110 per share and the September 105 calls are now priced at $8. You wake up to news that the DOW is down 300 points due to some overnight news about trade wars. You check your computer and find that XYZ is down $2 and is now trading at $108 with the September 105 calls trading at $7. You also discover that December 110 calls are also selling at $7. You decide that now is a good time to roll the position forward. You buy back the 10 September 105 calls at $7 (taking a $5 per option loss) and sell 10 December 110 calls at $7. Assuming that XYZ recovers to $110 per share by December expiration, you will have realized the following profit:

Original cost of XYZ: 1000 X $100 = -$100,000

Revenue from sale of 10 options = $2 X 100 X 10 = +$2000

Cost to repurchase 10 calls = $7 X 100 X 10 = -$7000

Revenue from sale of 10 options = $7 X 100 X 10 = +$7000

Proceeds from sale of XYZ = 1000 X $110 = +110,000

Profit (Loss) = $12,000

Percent Gain = 12% (6 mos.)

Annualized Gain = 24%

If you had stayed in your original position, and assuming that the price of XYZ was at least $105 at September expiration, you would have realized the following profit:

Original cost of XYZ: 1000 X $100 = -$100,000

Revenue from sale of 10 options = $2 X 100 X 10 = +$2000

Proceeds from sale of XYZ = 1000 X $105 = +105,000

Profit = $7,000

Percent Gain = 7% (3 mos.)

Annualized Gain = 28%

At first blush, it may appear from the annualized percentage gains that you would have been better off not rolling the position forward. However, that assumes that you will be able to find a new trade with the same favorable outcomes following the maturity of the initial position. Not all trades are equal. When you have a profitable trade in progress, there is generally merit in extending it even if the anticipated profits may not equal the sum of two lesser trades.

Characteristics of covered call positions:

- Max Profit = Premium Received - Purchase Price of Underlying + Strike Price of Short Call

- Max Profit Achieved When Price of Underlying $\geq$ Strike Price of Short Call

- Breakeven Point = Purchase Price of Underlying - Premium Received

- Loss Occurs When Price of Underlying < Purchase Price of Underlying - Premium Received

- Maximum Loss = Purchase Price of Underlying − Premium Received

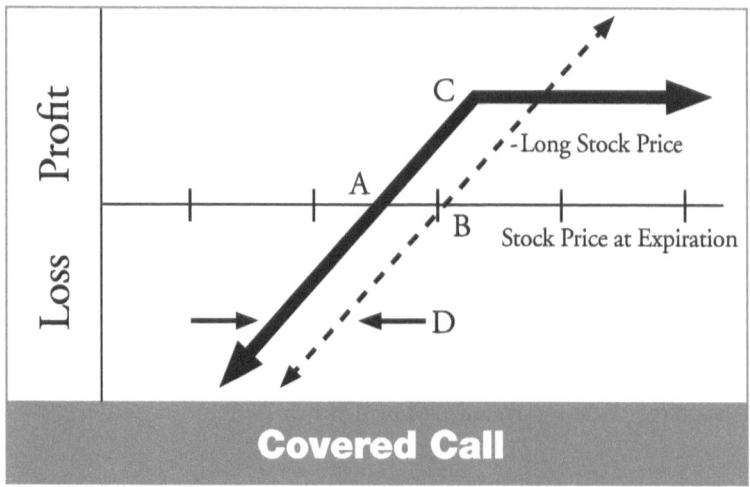

A. Break-even stock price at expiration
B. Original price paid for stock
C. Maximum profit
D. Downside protection

Summary

Myths about covered call writing:

1. Being assigned is bad

2. Forces investors to sell winners and keep losers

3. Covered writing is boring

4. Covered writing underperforms

Advantages:

1. Profit in trading (sideways) market

2. Earn maximum profit on position in a trading and rising market

3. Provides some measure of downside protection

4. Built-in sell strategy

5. Less volatile than buy and hold strategies

Covered-call writing is an appropriate strategy for conservative investors who anticipate that a stock will rise over time but are uncertain as to when that will happen or to what level. In covered call writing, the trader buys a stock (or ETF) that will profit if prices rally. The trader also sells a call option generally at a strike price above where the stock is currently trading and immediately receives the premium from the sale of this option. This premium income is retained regardless of what happens to the price of the stock. If stock prices remain static or decline, then the option will expire worthless and the premium received will help offset the loss, if any, on the long stock position. If prices rally beyond the strike price of the option by the time of the option expires, then the option will be exercised, and the long stock position will be closed automatically at the strike price. The maximum profit is the amount of the premium, plus the difference between the original stock price and the strike price, plus any dividends collected while holding the stock. The covered-call option writer will be happiest if at option expiration the stock is trading close to the strike price. If the stock price declines, she will be happier than if she had simply taken a long position in the stock and so long as the decline does not exceed the premium collected, she will suffer no loss with the trade. On the other hand, she will likely be unhappy if the stock price exceeds the strike price at expiration by more than the premium collected on the sale of the option. However even in this instance, she will have received the maximum profit she set out to achieve when she established the covered call position. No one ever went broke by taking maximum profits.

One word of warning. If the underlying stock pays dividends, then your short call may be exercised, and your stock assigned prior to expiration. The only time it would make sense for the contra party to exercise the call option would be for deep-in-the money calls a day or two before the stock goes ex-dividend.[18] So, with my covered call positions on ETFs, I consider rolling my in-the-money calls to the next or further out stock expiration date. Doing so also affords the opportunity to select a higher strike price at a reasonable cost. Obviously if the short call is out-of-the-money, it would make no sense for the contra party to exercise the option. In that case, I will either allow the call to expire worthless (and keep all the premium paid) or close the position and sell new calls with a future expiration date. For accounts such as IRAs which are required to be cash accounts as opposed to marginable accounts, you will not be able to sell additional calls until the existing ones are closed by expiration or by purchase.

---

[18] No prudent investor would exercise a call option with any significant time premium remaining of more than a day or two before the underlying stock is scheduled to go ex-dividend, although it does happen occasionally with amateur investors or investors who are in immediate need of cash (i.e. the kind of trading partner you like to find). In actuality, all option positions are held by clearing houses and mostly entered into by market makers who profit from the bid-ask spread. As a result, you never get to meet your actual victim!

CHAPTER EIGHT

Passive Option Writing Exceptional Returns

POWER

You're convinced, right? What can be better than a covered call strategy? If buying stock and simultaneously selling calls is the equivalent of selling puts, then why limit yourself to that one-sided bullish strategy? What if, for example, you're not bullish? What if you're ambivalent about market direction or agree with Burton Markiel that it is all a random walk? Why not sell an equal number of calls, which is a bearish strategy? Isn't the idea to profit from the sale of time premium? Why just sell puts? Selling both puts and calls is a market neutral strategy which performs best in a trading market and holds its own in a trending market – assuming the trend is not too strong. The long history of the stock market gives compelling proof that over time markets have trended to the upside, although certainly not by a straight line.

These charts illustrate why covered call strategies have been successful over time, although admittedly there have been corrections, recessions and short-term pull-backs over the years. Traders who consistently short the market face stiff head winds. The strategies that I employ as part of my POWER program involve the sale of equal numbers of at-the-money or near-the-money puts and calls but with a definite bias to the upside. Most frequently, the profits are realized on the short puts. However, even when the short calls expire in the money, the premium collected on the sale of the call offsets the loss on that position and there are many times when the profit is in the short call and not the short put.

If I am selling a straddle, I typically target a strike price that is somewhat higher than the current price of the underlying security. I use the same approach with short strangles with the lower strike (i.e. for the put) equal, to or slightly above current value, and the upper strike (i.e. for the call) somewhat above the current price of the underlying. With this approach, I have aligned myself with historical patterns. Another approach would be to sell more puts than calls, although this is not my preference.

The strategy will also work with options on individual securities. However, I prefer the diversification achieved from selling options on broad-based indices. While there is still market risk[19] in such strategy, we can avoid the stock risk[20] that comes from being concentrated in any particular security. Moreover, the volume of option trading in these popular ETFs assures greater liquidity of the options and tighter bid-ask spreads than with most individual securities. The strategy also can be used with cash indices such as the SPX, OEX, NDX, DJIA and RUT. However, these are cash-settled indices, which means that the holder of a long call has the right to exercise your short call option at any time and require you to accept cash for your short call (or in the case of the exercise of a short put, require you to pay cash). Why is this a problem? If you are called out of a position (or put into a cash position) by the exercise of the option by the holder, you will not be informed of the exercise until the following morning, in which case you will not be able to reestablish the position without the passage of some amount of time, during which the market may have moved against you.

Why is this not a problem with options on ETFs? While the holder of your short calls has the right to exercise at any time, as a practical matter a prudent person would only exercise early an in-the-money call on dividend-paying stocks on the day before the stock goes ex-dividend. Why? Because the owner of the call option wants to receive the dividend in addition to the stock. However, you will have benefited from receiving the strike price plus the premium collected and should be able to reestablish

---

[19] Market risk is the risk an investor or trader takes that a change in general economic conditions will affect the stock market in general.
[20] Stock risk is the risk that the stock price of a particular company will be affected by events specific to that company such as an FDA decision on a new drug.

your position under favorable terms because the stock will be marked down to reflect the payment of the dividend. Similarly, a prudent holder of a long put will only exercise a deep-in-the money put early in order to earn interest on the proceeds before expiration. But if you as the holder of a short put are assigned the underlying, you are in the same relative position as before the exercise because the delta of the short put and of the underlying are both +1. This is to say that for each point the market value increases, your gain on either position is the same. A one-point rise in the underlying will result in a one- point decrease in the value of the put (or one-point increase in the short put). As a result, you will find yourself in substantially the same position after you have been assigned on the exercise of the short put. In either case, you are hoping that the market will go up and you can reestablish your original position if you wish by selling the stock you were assigned and selling a new put, preferably with a more distant expiration and new at-the-money strike price. Because the underlying security you are assigned has the same delta as the short put you no longer hold, you are not affected by a change in market conditions as you very well could have been if dealing with cash-settled options. Why are the index options cash settled? The answer is because you can't buy an index.

Following are profit-loss profiles for short straddles and strangles. It should be noted that higher potential profits are attainable with the short straddle. However, the short strangle offers a wider profit range and slightly better breakeven points. While there is a possibility of a larger profit with the short straddle (when the stock price is pinned to the strike price at expiration), there are better odds of making a profit with the short straddle.

Breakeven Points – Here are the upside and downside breakeven points for the short straddle and strangle positions:

For Straddles:

- Breakeven Points = Strike Price $\pm$ Net Premium Received

For Strangles:

- Upper Breakeven Point = Strike Price of Short Call + Net Premium Received

- Lower Breakeven Point = Strike Price of Short Put - Net Premium Received

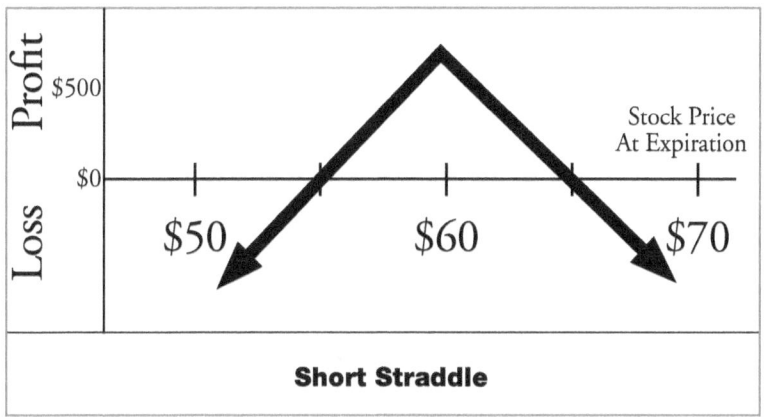

Short Straddle

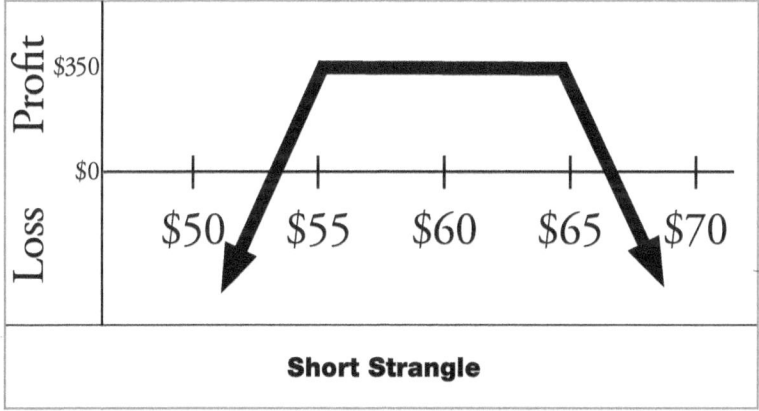

Short Strangle

For example, in April you sell a June straddle when XYZ stock is priced at $60. You receive $2.50 for the put and $2.50 for the call for a total of $500 ($2.50 X 100 + $2.50 X 100). Your maximum profit is $500. The downside breakeven point at expiration is $60 - $2.50 - $2.50 = $55. The upside breakeven point is $60 + $2.50 + $2.50 = $65.

Suppose instead you sell a June strangle receiving $1.75 for the $55 put + $1.75 for the $65 call. Now, the maximum profit is only $350. However, the breakeven points are more favorable. The downside breakeven is $55 - $1.75 - $1.75 = $51.50. The upside breakeven is $65 + $1.75 + $1.75 = $68.50.

While the profit potential for the straddle is greater than the strangle, the strangle offers a greater potential for profits. The decision whether to sell a straddle vs. strangle involves a tradeoff with the straddle being the more aggressive position.

Defensive Actions

As with any stock or option strategy, there is risk. Were it not so, investors would flock to the strategy in such large numbers to take away your secret advantage. Who in their right mind would invest in treasuries or CDs paying barely 1% annualized interest if a 15% return could be realized with similar risks? While risk of loss cannot be eliminated with any strategy involving options including the one I utilize, those risks can be reduced with timely defensive actions. When you establish a short straddle or strangle position, you are hoping for a stable or trading market. Due to being long theta, you will benefit from time decay and in most instances profit from your positions without the need to take any remedial action. Not so, if the market makes a big move up or down.

In fast moving markets, it is best to take defensive action to mitigate or avoid realizing significant losses. Not being one to chase after such markets, I generally like to wait for an opportune time to "roll" my positions forward. Fortunately, even strong trending markets or markets experiencing panic selling nearly always offer at least temporary reversals rather than move in a straight line. I consider such reversals an opportunity to roll out of what have become deep-in-the options. By rolling a losing put position diagonally down and out, we are able to reestablish our positions with a minimum of damage. Often by rolling out three months we are able to significantly mitigate our loss by selling time premium. And of course, if our short puts are deep-in-the-money, our short calls are nearly worthless, meaning that we will have earned a maximum return on the calls thereby allowing us to retain the full premium which serves as an additional offset against any loss on our put positions. The combination of selling time premium will mitigate any losses and often results in a break even or even profitable overall trade. When markets fall rapidly, implied volatility usually spikes, which increases the premium you receive when selling the more distant options. While volatility also affects that price of the short option, the effect is greater on the more distant option, which mitigates against the adverse effect of trending markets. The same approach can be used when the market moves upward by rolling the now in-the-money short calls to a more distant expiration with a higher strike price. While markets can move violently in either direction, up or down, historically bullish moves are more orderly than bearish ones.

Recognizing that markets can greatly fluctuate during turbulent times, I try not to join the herd and chase after it. By limiting individual bets and having adequate capital, I have always been able to weather the storms. As a general rule, I will look for opportunities to roll in-the-money options when their current value is 175% of my original position during the expiration month and then only on days when the market moves in my favor. Short-term options are more sensitive to changes in the price of the underlying than longer term options. By waiting to trade when the market is moving back in a more favorable direction, you are able to minimize the adverse effects of an adverse market.

When I first started to think about writing this book many years ago, I had planned to name it Passive Option Writing Easy Rules, using the catchy acronym POWER. At that time, I felt that predetermined or static trading rules should be utilized to avoid chasing the market or allowing emotions - fear and greed - to get in the way of making profits. Those rules required the POWER trader to hold positions until expiration regardless of market movements. Extensive back testing confirmed the profitability of such an automated static trading system. Over time, however, as I developed a "feel" for the market, I came to the conclusion that I could usually outperform a static approach with a more dynamic one that involved making adjustments as market conditions dictated. One of the major advantages of the static approach is that it minimizes the time needed to implement POWER. Once you put on the positions, you stand pat until expiration Friday when you realize your profits or losses and put on new positions. That system worked well for me especially when my time was limited due to my day job responsibilities. I never felt it fair to my employer to allow myself to be distracted by the stock market during working hours. By sticking with static rules, I had no need to follow the markets on an intraday basis. But as I scaled back on other responsibilities over the years, and had more free time, I was able devote more time to implementing trading strategies. At the same time, I acquired the experience and feel that goes with being a market watcher and discovered that I could increase profits by engaging in a more dynamic approach and making adjustments as changing market conditions dictated. Of course, there have been occasions where I would have been better off allowing the static rules to dictate trading decisions. However, over time, I became very confident of my ability to enhance profits by being proactive and less passive. That is when I decided to change the last two terms underlying the acronym, POWER, to Passive Option Writing *Exceptional Return* Strategy. While time decay is still at the center of my trading system, I have found it possible to enhance returns by adjusting my positions to market conditions and taking defensive action when warranted.

A Word of Caution

Remember, POWER is a probability-based trading strategy, not just another gambling system. By necessity, all trading strategies contain at least some level of risk. Were it not so, all sophisticated traders would have gravitated to the "easy money". Only U.S. Treasury securities and FDIC certificates of deposit (CDs) and savings accounts, are considered to be virtually free from market risk and are used as benchmarks for evaluating other investment proposals. Even these "safe investments" contain interest-rate risk. For that reason, comparisons are generally made with short-term instruments or with Treasuries and CDs having the same maturity.

In order to remove the gambling element from covered-call writing or from our POWER strategy, we need to unwind our short option positions as they reach expiration. Most stock options expire on the third Friday of the month (actually on Saturday but trading stops at the close of the market on Friday). To avoid gambling on market direction, you should consider rolling your option positions forward before the options expire. Otherwise, you risk an unfavorable market move over the weekend. With either covered calls or short straddles (strangles) you will automatically be taken out of your current option positions at expiration. In the case of covered calls, if the option is in the money (case no. 1), you will be automatically assigned and be left with only a cash position. With out-of-the money options (case no. 2), you will be left with your long stock position. So, what's the problem? If, in case no. 1, it is your intention to reestablish a new covered call position on Monday, you will be unhappy if the market spikes or trends upward over the weekend. The position you establish on Monday will be less desirable than the opportunity to do so on Friday. Of course, if the market dives over the weekend, you will be happy that you were called out of your position. With case no. 2, you will be unhappy if the market tanks over the weekend. The call you sell on Monday will be less valuable as the call you could have sold on Friday. If you wish to gamble, then being out of the market over the weekend is not a bad thing. As for me, I choose not to gamble. If that means that I occasionally lose the benefit of a market swing in my direction, I am ok with that knowing that over time the success or failure of my strategies is dependent on favorable odds, not the luck of the draw. That's also why I stay out of casinos. I am the "house". I count on repeated small wagers with the odds in my favor.

Similarly, with short straddles and strangles, I allow the out-of-the-money option to expire worthless. Remember, either the call or the put is guaranteed to expire worthless (unless pinned to the strike – more on that in a moment). If the put is in the money, I will wait until the close and either buy back the put so that it never gets exercised or roll it forward while at the same time establishing a new short call position with the same expiration. Interestingly, it is often possible to re-purchase the expiring short put for (or slightly below) its intrinsic value. This is because traders holding long puts at expiration are often willing to sell them at any price creating a trading imbalance which creates an opportunity for buyers like us. On the other hand, with respect to my short calls, my preference is to purchase enough shares of the underlying stock just prior to the close with the knowledge that the holder of my short call options will exercise the right to purchase those shares from me. In other words, what I will have accomplished by this maneuver is to convert my short call position to a covered call position. In so doing, I will have avoided paying for any time premium which calls retain into the closing.

You should be aware that while stock trading stops at 4 pm ET, options can be traded for up to 15 minutes after the close or until 4:15 pm ET. That 15 minutes can give option traders an advantage over stock traders, especially where there is an announcement after the close that affects the market. Once again, such after-market moves in option prices may work both for and against you. As a result, being true to our non-gambling mentality, it is generally wise to make your option trades as soon after 4 pm as possible. If the market moves in an unfavorable direction after the close, you have the opportunity to improve your position by scaling into it, which I discuss in Chapter 13.

CHAPTER NINE

The Greeks

No respectable author of an options book can avoid talking about the "Greeks". And I don't mean Aristotle and Socrates. No, I'm referring to Greek letters such as delta, gamma, theta and vega (whoops, vega is not a Greek letter but is treated as such in options books to describe volatility).

    Rather than put you to sleep or lose you by explaining the nuances of the Greeks, I would prefer to highlight what you need to know about them to be a successful option trader. The most important Greek for our purposes is alpha. Alpha is the measure of performance on a risk-adjusted basis. Alpha takes the volatility or price risk of an investment and compares its risk-adjusted performance to a benchmark index. The excess return of the fund relative to the return of the benchmark index is a fund's alpha.[21] The most common benchmark is the S&P 500 index. We saw above that most time periods a buy-write strategy outperformed the S&P 500 index with less risk and volatility. I would submit that a put-call selling strategy can enhance both results. There is nothing like being an alpha male or female.

---

[21] www.investopedia.com/terms/a/alpha.asp

Next in importance is delta or Δ. Delta is a forecast of how a directional change in the underlying will affect the price of an option. Delta measures directional risk and is an estimation of the change in the price of the option given a one unit move in the price of the underlying stock. Delta has a positive value for call options ranging from 0 to 1.0. A deep in-the-money call will have a delta of close to 1.0. For each $1 increase in the stock, the option increases nearly $1 as well. A far out-of-the money call will have a delta approaching 0 meaning that the option hardly moves with increases in the stock price. Conversely, delta is always negative for puts. A deep-in-the-money put has a value approaching -1.0. As the stock declines in price a deep-in-the-money put tags along dollar for dollar.

As an option seller you would prefer that the market sits still and allows both option positions to decay with the passage of time. As such you prefer to be "delta neutral" or have a net delta position of 0. A short straddle initiated when the stock is at the strike price will have a delta of 0. The call will have a delta of +.5 and the put a delta of -.5 which together equal a delta of 0. The overall delta of the position is determined by adding the call delta to the put delta. An increase in the underlying will be no more welcome to the straddle seller than a decrease. If the stock increases in value today causing our combined delta position to move into positive territory, we are hoping for a decline in stock values tomorrow. If the stock price hovers around the strike price or returns to that position prior to expiration, we are going to profit. Our margin of error is equal to the strike price ± the total premium collected. So, for example, if we sell a $50 call for $1.50 and a $50 put for $1.50 with the same expiration date, we will profit if the stock closes on expiration between $47.00 and $53.00.

If during the holding period of the option position, the delta of the position has moved close to 1.0 or -1.0, we need to think about readjusting our position. For me, if my combined position is -0.75 < delta < 0.75, I am generally willing to stand pat with my position in the hope that it swings back closer to the middle range preferably to delta neutral or 0. If the combined option position exceeds the limits that I have set, I look for an opportunity to roll the entire position forward to a future expiration month. This requires me to close the current positions and reestablish new positions in the more distant month with a delta of 0. With any luck, the positions that I rolled out of will have still earned a small profit or at least not lost significant money. This is often the case where you have held the position for a period. While one leg of rollout will be entered at a loss, the other leg will be entered at a profit, and with the decay of time premium on both legs, the trade will at least break even most of the time with an opportunity to profit from the new delta neutral position. More about this later. Gamma is the rate of change of the delta as the underlying price changes. While gamma can be a useful concept for professional traders, the complexity and uses of the concept are beyond the scope of this text.

The following diagram demonstrates the relationship between a short straddle and its delta as the price of the underlying stock changes. Here the straddle with a strike price of 50 was sold 60 days prior to expiration when the stock was trading at 50, with the puts and calls selling for $3 each. As the price of the underlying stock increases beyond the strike price, the Δ of the position will decline, until reaching -1.0. Thereafter, as the price of the stock increases, the short straddle position will lose $1.00 for every $1.00 increase in the price of the stock (and initially gain $1.00 for every $1.00 decrease in the price of the stock). Conversely, as the price of the underlying stock declines below the strike price, the Δ of the short straddle increases until reaching +1.0. As the price of the stock decreases further, the position will lose $1.00 for every $1.00 decline in the price of the stock (and initially gain $1.00 for every $1.00 increase in the stock price). I use the term "initially" because the rate of gains or losses will diminish as Δ moves back toward zero. With short straddles profits are maximized when Δ is at or near zero. Conversely, long straddles maximize returns when Δ approaches -1.0 on the downside or +1.0 on the upside. A short straddle with a Δ of +1.0 is the functional equivalent of a long position in the underlying stock. As the stock price further declines, the short straddle follows along with dollar for dollar losses. A short straddle with a Δ of -1.0 is the functional equivalent of a short position in the underlying stock. In either instance the time premium of the options will have evaporated. The holder of a short straddle wants the stock price to remain at or move back toward the strike price.

When Δ moves substantially away from its beginning neutral position (+/- 0.75), it is advisable to make adjustments to reemploy the edge provided by the POWER strategy and to take advantage of time decay. Failure to do so results in you taking the same speculative position as that of stock investors, whether long or short.

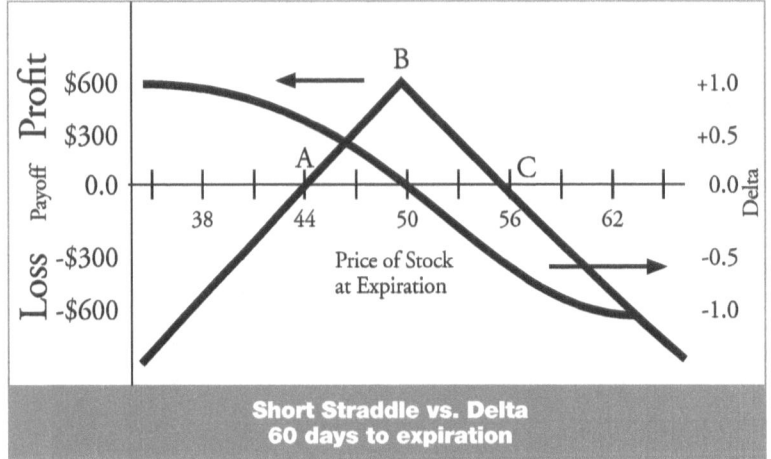

**Short Straddle vs. Delta
60 days to expiration**

A. Downside break-even point
B. Maximum profit when Δ = O
C. Upside break-even point

For an excellent in-depth analysis of volatility, I commend you to Sheldon Natenberg's *Option Volatility & Pricing*.[22] Professor Natenberg has long been recognized as a leading expert on volatility. For our purposes, it is sufficient to point out that volatility refers to the pricing of options. An option's price is equal to its intrinsic value plus the time premium. The time premium component is comprised of the time remaining to expiration and the volatility of the underlying security. The greater the expectation of price changes and the further off the expiration date, the greater the time premium and the more expensive the option. Since market participants establish the market price for the option, we can easily determine the amount of the option price that is attributable to the intrinsic value of the

---

[22] Sheldon Natenberg (2015). *Option Volatility & Pricing* (2nd ed.). New York, NY: McGraw-Hill

option and the amount due to the time premium. Historical volatility is backward looking and is based on the actual price changes in the preceding 12 months. Implied volatility, on the other hand, is forward looking and is expressed in terms of the anticipated annualized change in the price of the underlying stock in the next 12 months. For a stock with a current price of 100 and an implied volatility of 15, the expectation is that there is a 2/3 probability (one standard deviation) that the stock will trade between 85 and 115 during the next 12 months. During the next month, the expectation is that the stock will trade between 95.67 and 104.33, and during the next week between 97.92 and 102.08. Of course, these are only expectations. A full one-third of the time, the stock is expected to trade outside of these ranges and only after the fact can we know the actual price fluctuation or the historical volatility. While historical volatility is backward looking, implied volatility is forward looking. To maximize profits from our option selling we want to look for situations where the implied volatility exceeds the historical volatility. As we have seen previously, those opportunities are most frequently presented during periods of market fear represented by market selloffs.

For those wanting to do your own calculations of monthly, weekly or daily implied volatility, remember that the published implied volatility is given as an annualized number. For the monthly, weekly and daily implied volatilities, you would simply multiply the annual number by factors of 0.288, 0.139, and 0.0625, respectively.

What about periods of relative market tranquility, i.e. when the historical volatility exceeds the implied volatility? This situation generally occurs during periods of market complacency which is often followed by a steep selloff. Because we are matching our sale of puts with the sale of calls, the interdependency of the two positions may still offer a trading edge to option sellers. However, I try not to make a practice of selling options with historical volatilities greater than the implied. In such situations, I sit on the sideline and keep my powder dry. Experience has taught me that my patience will be rewarded. When the selloff comes, as it always does, I am prepared to search for selling opportunities that will fit in my overall option portfolio (more on that subject later).

Thomas J. Homer, JD, CFP®

The theta of an option is the rate at which the time premium of the option decays over time. Theta varies depending on whether the option is in the money or out of the money. Option sellers are long theta. The rate of decay of time premium accelerates as we approach expiration. Theta is greatest for at-the-money options and increases in value as the option approaches expiration when the value of theta theoretically approaches infinity. This is just a fancy way of explaining that at expiration, the time value of the option disappears. What does all this mean to the option seller? It means that the most desirable options to sell are at-the-money, short-term options (30 to 90 days). In my practice, I look for at-the-money options with 90 days or less until expiration. This strategy allows me take full advantage of being long theta. Because I am selling both at-the-money puts and calls, I will earn maximum profits if the price of the underlying remains unchanged at the time of expiration. My break-even point when selling a straddle is the strike price $\pm$ the total premium collected. If the strike price is 100 and the combined premium of the puts and calls is 5, I will make a profit if at expiration the stock price is $95 \leq X \leq 105$. For strangles, I have an even larger breakeven range, being the total premium minus the put strike price on the downside and the total premium plus the call strike price on the upside. At expiration, theta = ∞ and time premium = 0, as the option price merges with its intrinsic value.

So, in our example where we sold a put and call, collecting $5 premium, on a $100 stock with a strike price of $100, we will have earned $250 for each straddle sold for a stock which closes on expiration day at $102.50. While this may seem like a paltry sum, the accumulated profits from several overlapping option positions can provide exceptional results over the long term. While the strategy may not be glitzy in the eyes of the speculator, the consistent profits attained over a prolonged period will be the envy of portfolio managers everywhere, a full two-thirds of whom fail to beat the S&P 500.

Maximizing Theta Decay

Time decay in options accelerates as they approach expiration. Upon expiration, options lose all of their time value. At that moment, out-of-the-money options expire worthless while in-the-money options assume their intrinsic value. Longer-term options, such as LEAPS lose very little value on a daily basis. Therefore, as a seller of options, it generally makes sense to sell options with only a short time remaining until expiration. The following graph illustrates the rate of decay over a 90-day period. Some option traders may logically favor selling only near-term options since decay accelerates during the last 30 days. However, transaction costs compared to the relatively small premiums remaining 30 days out often make such short-term trades unattractive. My personal preference is to initiate positions 90 days from expiration. As options expire, I sell new ones 90 days from expiration. In this way, upon each expiration date, I am generally holding short option positions which will expire in 90, 60, and 30 days. This strategy employs the concepts of diversification and laddering.

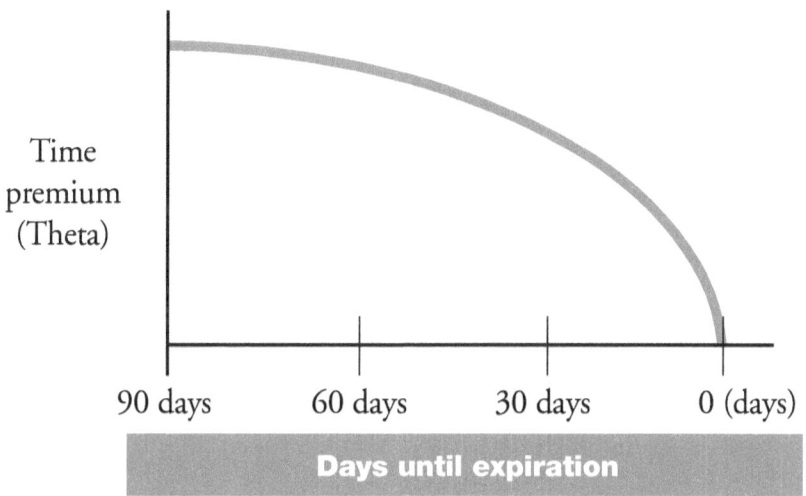

Sellers of options are "long theta" while buyers are "short theta". Theta is the dollar amount an option seller earns on a daily basis without any other market changes (i.e. static market price and implied volatility values). Since all options lose time value as time passes, the theta of an option is usually expressed as a negative number.

For example, an option with a theta value of -0.10, will lose 0.10 of value each day that passes with no movement in the price of the underlying stock (all attributable to a loss of time premium). In three days, the option will have lost 0.30 of time premium in a static market. Such an option worth $5.00 on Tuesday will be worth $4.70 on Friday. In actuality, theta moves in a non-linear manner accelerating into expiration at which time the option loses all of its time premium value, leaving only the intrinsic value of the option.

CHAPTER TEN

Market Timing is Dangerous

"Successful market timing requires two correct decisions: when to get out and when to get back in. Guessing right once is a 50/50 proposition. Guessing right twice drops the odds to only 25 percent. One wrong guess and you shoot yourself in one foot; two wrong guesses and you shoot yourself in both feet."[23]

---

[23] Ferri, R. *Forbes* 6/12/2014

Thomas J. Homer, JD, CFP®

Let's get one thing straight. The stock market is volatile. With absolutely no warning, the market can implode by 10% or more in a very short period. A decline of 10% is considered a correction. A decline of 20% signals a recession. Following such a dramatic change, prognosticators are quick to give the reasons. Perhaps, it was due to an unfavorable jobs report, a speech by the Federal Reserve Chairman or a member of the Federal Reserve Board of Governors, reports of an economic slowdown in China or Greece, a sharp incline or decline in oil prices, etc. etc. Interestingly, those same prognosticators failed to predict the selloff in advance and for good reason. Often bad news on the economic front, such as higher unemployment, leads simultaneously to concerns about a slowdown and investor optimism that the Fed will lower or hold the line on interest rates. If the market has moved down, it's because of the slowdown. If it moves higher, it's because of an accommodative Federal Reserve. Trouble is, you weren't warned as to how the market will react to these events. It always seems so apparent as to what was about to happen when the commentators attempt to explain what has just occurred. What is often missed is the fact that the market may have been poised for a correction and that the events leading up to the event had little if anything to do with it. Hindsight being 20-20, we agonize over our failure to see the storm coming. It seems so clear now based on the reasons advanced for the move. "If I had only sold my stocks yesterday or last week, I could have avoided the pain I am now feeling. How could I be so stupid?" The problem is that no one had a crystal ball. Sure, there will always be those who point out that they predicted what was about to happen. But that is more a function of the fact that at any given time there are both bulls and bears, so one of the camps is always going to be correct if just by happenstance. If you're inclined to listen to your favorite analyst, you may be better off doing the opposite.

When advisor sentiment reaches bullish or bearish extremes, the smart money bets against the majority view. *Investors Intelligence* measures investor sentiment. This survey has been widely adopted by the investment community as a contrarian indicator and is followed closely by the financial media. Since its inception in 1963, the indicator has a consistent record for predicting major market turning points. The norm is when advisors are

45% bullish, 35% bearish, and 20% neutral.[24] When this 10-point spread between bulls and bears widens to extreme levels, it may be time to sell. Conversely, when the bears overtake the bulls by a wide margin, it may be time to buy. The theory is when most investors are already bullish, most of the available cash has already been invested. During the October 2007 market peak the bulls outpaced the bears by a stunning margin of 42.4% (four times the norm).[25] You don't need to be reminded of the direction the market took thereafter.

Our human instincts cause us to believe that the current trends will continue indefinitely into the future. As a result, we believe we know what the future portends. Such thinking can and often does lead to large losses in the stock market.

As markets go up, whether stocks, commodities, or real estate, investors tend to become overly bullish and grow complacent. Conversely, as markets go down, investors tend to become overly pessimistic. I believe this natural human condition traces its origins to the caveman era. In times of good weather, plentiful game, and tranquil conditions, people became less fearful and adventuresome. During adverse conditions, they tended to hunker down in their caves. Such behavioral adaptations no doubt made sense and led to better chance for survival. However, that same instinctive behavior can have disastrous results for investors.

The following pictorial illustrates the cycle of market emotions which all traders experience. If we allow our actions to be guided by our emotions, we will inevitably make the wrong decisions at just the wrong times.

---

[24] Source CBOE
[25] Alan Abelson writing in Barrons in early 2011

Thomas J. Homer, JD, CFP®

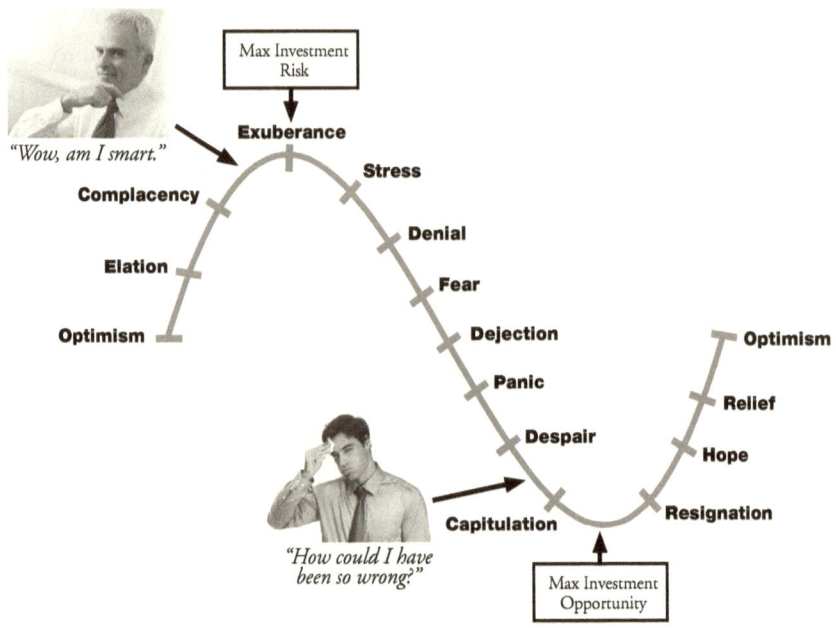

We are all familiar with the trader's credo "the trend is your friend". But how can that be reconciled with the contrarian point of view? Who among us dares to argue with Warren Buffet who has consistently mastered the art of buying low and selling high? After all, it was Buffet who wisely proclaimed, "Most people get interested in stocks when everyone else is. The time to get interested is when no one else is. You can't buy what is popular and do well."

The truth is that stocks can definitely follow trends for long periods of time, whether up, down, or sideways. Technicians make their living following trends and then calling reversals, which are inevitable occurrences in the stock market. The key to successful trading is to be in sync with the market. Think of the beauty of a skillful jockey galloping on his mount in perfect up and down rhythm. Successful stock traders are those who learn the art of riding the waves of an often-turbulent sea. Knowing when to use the whip and when to brake is an art which one acquires only after years of stock market observation. Whether you rely on fundamental analysis, technical indicators, or your gut, it is essential to your long-term success in beating the indices that your trading activity is in harmony with the overall market.

One of the greatest impediments to successful trading is having a healthy mental attitude. Too many traders vacillate between exuberance and despair and allow their decisions to be influenced by their moods. We have all heard the stories about traders jumping off of tall buildings on October 24, 1929 "Black Thursday". During the 2008–09 financial crisis, stories abounded of suicide, alcoholism, divorce, and general dysfunctionality among many money managers and traders. Some later told stories of refusing to watch television, take calls from clients, or even look at their portfolios. Better to be in a state of denial than to deal with devastating reality. Many of the survivors of that uber-stressful period are now driving for Uber, selling clothes, or engaged in other lines of work–not that there is anything wrong with those activities.

Market news should not be feared or dreaded but rather looked upon as presenting opportunity. If you awaken to news of a major overnight market implosion, be thankful that you have been presented with the opportunity to put idyll cash to work at favorable prices or to roll out of a losing short call position. If the market is up, consider taking profits or repositioning oversold positions. Negative thinking and unwillingness to take a loss are the trader's biggest enemies.

Some years ago, I took a graduate course in commodities and futures at the Illinois Institute of Technology Stuart School of Business that was taught by Professor Howard Simons. It was an interesting course and leading to my successful passage of the National Commodity Futures Examination, otherwise known as the Series 3 exam. In discussing behavioral tendencies of traders, Professor Simons argued that traders often become risk averse in the realm of gains and risk-seeking in the realm of loss. According to Professor Simons, this tendency explained the reluctance of traders to "take a loss". He argued that the act of taking losses makes people feel depressed, believe that the markets are rigged against them, are naturally unlucky, or are personal failures. While traders may be inclined to cash in on their winnings they are reluctant to cash out on their losses. Casino owners and gamblers might offer a case study. When gamblers are losing they often keep playing in the hopes of erasing those losses. As a result, small losses often become large ones. The same is true of traders. Often, it is better to cut your losses, learn from the experience, and live to fight another day.

Behavioral economics has advanced a phenomenon called "Prospect Theory" to explain how decision making is influenced by the desire to avoid a loss.[26] People don't like taking losses. Consider the following choice:

> Decision # 1 — (A) 100% chance of winning $3000 vs (B) 80% chance of winning $4000 but with a 20% chance of winning nothing. Statistically the expected value of A is $3000 while the expected value of B is $3200. Yet, field trials show that 80% of people chose Option A.

> Decision # 2 — (A) 100% chance of losing $3000 vs (B) 80% chance of losing $4000 but a 20% chance of losing nothing. The expected value of A is ($3000) while the expected value of B is ($3200). A full 92% of those tested chose Option B.

At least three conclusions can be reached as a result of this exercise: (1) people don't like experiencing losses, (2) people tend to overweight small probabilities and underweight large ones; and (3) people like certainty.

A successful trader must be able to deal with adversity. Markets go up and come down. There are going to be rough periods no matter what your trading strategy. Learning to take a loss is the single hardest and most important lesson that a trader has to master. Markets are dynamic. The next profitable opportunity is just around the corner. Sometimes you just have to clear the deck in order to move forward. Denial leading to inaction resulting in confusion and anger are toxic. Get over it!

---

[26] Shortridge, Kelly, Behavioral Models of InfoSec: Prospect Theory https://medium.com/@kshortridge/behavioral-models-of-infosec-prospect-theory-c6bb49902768

CHAPTER ELEVEN

Living the Wisdom of the Tao

"In Chines philosophy, Tao is the absolute principle underlying the universe, combining within itself the principles of yin and yang and signifying the way, or code of behavior, that is in harmony with the natural order."[27]

As noted in the previous chapter, it is essential that traders neither respond to market volatility with impulsive reactions, not be lulled into complacency by rising markets. Rather a successful trader understands that both conditions are normal market activity and will be prepared to act in harmony with the market as conditions change.

In this book *The Tao of Trading*[28], Robert Koppel explains the "Samurai Psyche" of successful traders by identifying the following shared attributes of top traders:

---

[27] English Oxford Living Dictionaries, *https://en.oxforddictionaries.com/definition/tao*
[28] Robert Koppel (1998). *The Tao of Trading*, Chicago, IL, Dearborn Financial Publishing

- They understand their motives for trading.

- They develop trading strategies that work for them because they fit their personalities

- They enjoy trading and make it effortless

- They work hard at developing their skills and maintaining a trading edge

- They trade with total confidence in themselves and their methodology

- They trade in a positive state of mind that allows them the flexibility to act automatically and know exactly the next right step to take in the market.

- They intuitively understand money management and risk control and know that no single trade is worth everything.

- They have a strategy that works and the discipline to carry it out.

- They are independent thinkers and understand that they are personally responsible for all market decisions.

- They understand the difference between loss and losing.

- They understand the importance of acting at difficult times with circumscribed risk.

- They know what drives markets and the difference between hope and fear.

- They don't trade to please others.

During my option trading career, I have found it useful and at times reassuring to rely on the analysis of one or more external advisors for major market turns. Anyone who has closely followed the stock market over a long period of time, will note the existence of long-term trends. There are structural Bull and structural Bear markets, which can be very long term, and cyclical Bull and Bear markets which can and do exist within both. The current bull market on an annualized basis through the current date (December 2018), has witnessed the S&P 500 has gaining 16.5% since March 2009, this is spite of a very volatile end-of-year market. The longest bull run before this one began in October 1990 and ended with the bursting of the dotcom bubble in March 2000. During all of those turbulent times, I have placed considerable reliance on one such external advisor. Bob Brinker, host of the nationally syndicated radio program, *Money Talk*, and author of the Marketimer monthly newsletter, has been a steady source of reliable market predictability. For the most part, Brinker has been a very reliable forecaster of major market turns. Brinker's market timing model engages in both fundamental and technical analysis with a heavy reliance on historical trends for market entry and exit signals. On the fundamental side, monetary and fiscal policies are examined along with interest rates (including the slope of the interest rate curve), inflationary trends, growth rates, and an over or under valuation analysis. On the technical side, Investor sentiment is taken into account with a contrarian point of view. Consideration is also given to historical factors such as traditional off-year presidential election trends for pull-backs in the stock market of 10% or more. While Brinker's trade signals are very infrequent, Marketimer gave a sell signal in January 2000 near market highs and a buy signal in 2003 near market lows. The publication was less helpful in calling market highs in 2007 but has made a number of other correct calls over the years. Because of its deliberative and unemotional analysis during periods of market volatility, I have found Marketimer to provide reassuring analysis. Such advice encourages support for a steady course and to avoidance of panic selling during market declines. In every market crisis there is no shortage of so-called experts who proclaim, in the words of Redd Foxx as he grabbed his heart, "this is the big one, Elizabeth, I'm coming to join you!"[29] You are well-advised to avoid following such advice.

---

[29] *Sanford and Son*, NBC sitcom (1972-77).

Thomas J. Homer, JD, CFP®

    There are other noteworthy analysts, who bring the same type of calm deliberative analysis to the subject of market projections. Maybe for you it is Jim Cramer, host of CNBC's "Mad Money" and co-anchor of "Squawk on the Street". While he can be a little eccentric and overly demonstrative for my tastes, Cramer is very often correct in his market predictions. My good friend and option trading expert, Professor Jim Bittman, follows Michael Cintolo, chief analyst of the Cabot Growth Investor newsletter. No matter the shortcomings and limitations inherent in market timing, I have found it comforting and useful to be able to turn to one or more trusted advisor during those unsettling times of extreme volatility in the markets. After all, we are only human and need a reassuring hug from time to time. Regardless, we can find comfort in knowing that in the 200-year history of the stock market, no singular event, such as the Great Depression, two world wars, 9-1-1, or the 2008 financial crisis have had a lasting impact on the stock market, contrary to wide-spread predictions of financial Armageddon at the time.

    As you begin to understand and accept the ebbs and flows of the stock market and the cycle of market emotions, you will be able to experience a calmness during periods of market volatiliy – the Samurai Psyche. Down days in the market will be opportunity days, rather than dreaded events. You will be living the wisdom of the Tao!

CHAPTER TWELVE

Sure Bets

The conventional wisdom among financial professionals holds that when it comes to investments, there is no such thing as a sure bet. Investment returns are compared to the risk-free rate of return, which is based on US Treasury Bills. In order to earn a greater return, you must be prepared to accept risk – the greater the risk the higher the expected return – and the greater potential for loss. It has always amazed me how many people believe that there are risk-free ways to earn a higher return than that provided by treasuries. Markets are efficient. If there is an investment that yields a high rate of return without risk, money managers and professional traders would be all over it. The result of the demand for such products, would be to drive the rates down to the level being generated by treasuries. There is no such thing as a free ride when it comes to investment strategies!

Fool's Gold

One common "sure bet" promoted by some stock brokers and financial advisors is referred to as the "dividend capture strategy". This strategy involves the purchase and sell of dividend-paying stocks just prior to and immediately following the stock's ex-dividend date. Most such stocks declare dividends quarterly payable to investors who own the stock as of a specified date, known as the ex-dividend date. The ex-dividend date is usually two business days before the record date. If you purchase a stock on or after its ex-dividend date, you will not receive the dividend payment. Instead, the seller will. However, if you purchase the stock the day before the ex-dividend date, you get the dividend. Proponents of this strategy suggest buying a dividend-paying stock a day or two before it goes ex-dividend and selling the stock on or soon after it goes ex-dividend. That way, the theory holds, you can earn a free dividend. This strategy assumes that the stock price will not decline during the holding period. The problem with the strategy is that it seldom works. Stock exchanges automatically lower the stock's price by the amount of the dividend on the ex-dividend date. As a result, you are likely to lose the same amount on the price of the stock as you earned with the extra dividend, and you will have paid two commissions for the privilege.

If you hold a covered call position or the equivalent short put position in a stock, you may well find that your counter party will exercise his option two days in advance of the ex-dividend date in order to acquire the right to the dividend. As a result, you may be tempted to close the short option position to protect against such exercise and assignment, which might make sense so that you can avoid being out of the market and having to re-establish a new position, incurring new transaction costs. In this scenario, you would be reacting to players of the dividend capture strategy even though the strategy may have only illusory benefits. As a result, I often roll such short option positions forward before the counter party has the opportunity to "mess with my position".[30]

While I concur that there are no free rides, I have discovered a few investment strategies that come close. One of those is detailed in previous chapters. Selling options takes advantage of natural conditions that exist in financial markets where participants act somewhat irrationally due

---

[30] Other potential situations where you may be assigned on your short option position are described in Chapter 13.

to greed (speculators) and fear (hedgers), which make such participants willing victims in the game of trading. Such participants are willing to give you their money for reasons unrelated to the probabilities of winning the trade. Just as casino operators and insurance companies profit from such individuals, so can you through option selling as explained in this book.

However, I have discovered three investment strategies that come very close to being sure things. One involves selling volatility, one selling distant deep-in-the money (ITM) puts, and another buying discounted CDs and other fixed income instruments.

Selling Volatility

The most popular volatility index is the VIX, or the Chicago Board Options Exchange Market Volatility Index, which measures the implied volatility of S&P 500 index options.[31] The VIX is a measure of volatility based on options trades and expectations of stock market volatility over the next 30-day period.

As discussed in Chapter 2, market volatility significantly influences option prices. It has long been understood by researchers and professional traders that market fear can be quantified by the VIX. When the market drops sharply, the "fear index" tends to spike. Conversely, big up days in the stock market can be expected to result in a corresponding decline in the VIX. VIX also tends to decline during periods of market complacency, or during periods of "trading" rather than "trending" markets. Some traders use VIX as an indicator of when to become long or short. They believe that a low VIX is predictive of a sharp selloff in stocks. A high VIX portends a market rally.

The problem is that the VIX can and often does remain overbought or oversold (less common) for months at a time. While many market selloffs

---

[31] The first VIX index, based on the S&P 100 was introduced by the CBOE in 1993. Later, following CBOE trademark dispute resolutions, VIX was modified to measure volatility on the S&P 500.

take place during periods of low VIX, resulting in spikes in the VIX, it is not a reliable predictor of when that selloff will occur. So, while a sharp market implosion almost always results in a spike in the VIX, a low VIX is an ineffective market timing indicator. Said another way, while there is a definite correlation between stock prices and VIX, VIX is a lagging indicator, which is often of little use for market timing. When the stock market is trending higher, the VIX tends to drop. During market selloffs or crashes, VIX nearly always spikes. While this well-known correlation provides an opportunity for traders to hedge their bets, money can be lost waiting for the tide to turn. Being long volatility (i.e. owning VIX futures) has for the most part proven to be an ineffective hedge against falling stock market prices.

Moreover, there is an issue of how best to trade the VIX. The first VIX index, based on the S&P 100 was introduced by the CBOE in 1993, was not tradeable. Although VIX futures were introduced in 2003, they proved to be an ineffective hedge. Retail investors were often uncomfortable using the unfamiliar futures market to hedge a stock portfolio.

Following the financial crisis of 2008 and accompanying steep losses in the stock market, a new product, VXXB (VXX for the first 10 years), was introduced in January 2009. VXXB trades like an ETF even though it is not an exchange traded fund. Rather, it is an exchanged traded note (ETN) due to the fact that it is based on VIX futures which do not have a spot price. VXXB was an immediate success. Traders, investors and money managers, burned by the recent losses, sought investments which could provide an effective hedge against falling stock prices. VXXB offered that prospect. VXXB soon reached volumes not previously heard of for ETFs, even the popular ones like SPY, QQQ, IWM and DIA. Many investors purchased VXXB to protect against spikes in volatility. If only VXXB had been available for purchase pre-crash, the carnage could have been minimized! Or at least, so was the conventional wisdom at the time.

Fast forward to 2014 and we see that VXXB had lost over 99% of its value since inception. Wait it gets worse! By the end of 2017, VXXB had lost 99.9% of its original value. Larry Connors of Trading Market fame explains how VXXB is "built to go to zero". To date the VXXB price has been reset five times, utilizing 1 for 4 reverse stock splits, implemented in order to artificially pump up the price. If you owned 1000 shares of VXXB when the price was $10 per share, following a split, you would now own 250 shares at $40 per share. The issuers of ETFs, or in this case ETNs, make money when the trading volume remains high. Reverse stock splits are a way of accomplishing that objective. Investors are likely to be scared off when share prices continue to migrate downward with only occasional up ticks. As explained by Mr. Connors, there are two immutable reasons why VXXB is a losing bet. The first is the contango effect, and the second is the insurance effect. These are discussed below.

Contango

VIX futures markets are often in a state of contango[32], meaning that distant futures are almost always more expensive than those closer to expiration. At the short end of the maturity curve, the contango can be quite steep. That means that the "roll yield" incurred when selling expiring contracts and simultaneously purchasing next-month futures can be steep, creating a significant gap between a futures-based VIX and the hypothetical return on a spot investment in the VIX. (It should be noted that it is not possible to trade a spot market price on the VIX. VIX is a forward-looking value based on expectations). I realize that the concept of contango can be a bit confusing. However, what you need to know is that (1) VIX futures are almost always in a state of contango, and (2) the price to roll VXXB forward from the near to next term future is expensive, resulting in downward pressure on the price. Every 30 days, VXXB issuers basically sell low and buy high, not exactly a formula you want to buy into.

---

[32] As explained in Investopedia, Contango is a situation where the futures price of a commodity is above the expected spot price. Contango refers to a situation where the future spot price is below the current spot price, and people are willing to pay more for a commodity at some point in the future than the actual expected price of the commodity. This may be due to people's desire to pay a premium to have the commodity in the future rather than paying the costs of storage and the carry costs of buying the commodity today.

Cost of Insurance

Just as people are willing to overpay for homeowner's insurance, in order to enjoy peace of mind (and comply with lender requirements), traders and money managers are willing to overpay for the protection that VXXB affords in times of steep market selloffs. They are more than willing to sacrifice overall return for protection against taking a huge hit due to a black swan event[33]. A black swan, according to noted author Nassam Taleb, is a totally unpredictable event that can have a massive impact. After all, who has ever seen a black swan? Money managers get fired or sued for sustaining big losses regardless of the reason. Wouldn't you be willing to sacrifice performance for job security? But that just means that whoever takes the opposite side of the volatility trade is very likely to profit. It might as well be you. This is one of the few opportunities to outwit the experts, and they are willing victims!

Once convinced that being long VXXB is a losing proposition, how can you profit from that knowledge? The easiest way is to short VXXB. However, there are limits to such a strategy. For one thing, you have to be able to "borrow" shares of VXXB from your broker in order to be able to short it, and your broker needs to have shares to loan in the form of long positions. Although VXXB is widely traded, your broker may place limits on your ability to short it. Moreover, most investors are reticent to carry large short positions. Another possibility is to buy VXXB puts. But then you will have the headwinds of time decay to deal with. My preferred method to capitalize on this trade is to sell VXXB calls. Not only are the head winds in your favor, but so is time. As we have already seen with our option selling strategies, time is your friend. Moreover, VXXB options usually trade at high premiums due to high implied volatility (IV), which nearly always exceeds its historical volatility by a substantial margin.

This combination of favorable factors makes this strategy nearly foolproof and a consistent revenue producer. In the absence of a black swan event, you will profit handsomely from selling calls on the VXXB

---

[33] Taleb. N. (2010). *The Black Swan*. New York, NY: Random House Publishing Group.

because of the: (1) downward pressure on VXXB due to contango, and (2) willingness of traders to overpay for insurance by being long volatility, hence high implied volatility and time decay. To protect against the possibility of a black swan event, a risk-adverse trader will sell bearish call credit spreads (also called short-call spreads) rather than selling naked calls. This means that you will sell at-the-money (ATM) calls and buy the same number of out-of-the-money (OTM) calls with the same expiration dates. The price of such OTM calls is an affordable and reasonable cost of doing business. Similarly, a trader could buy a bearish put debit spread (also called a long-put spread) by buying ATM put options and selling OTM puts with the same expiration dates. Both of these strategies make money if VXXB stays the same or declines in value.

In either case, both the potential profit and loss are the same.

Examples:

A. *Bearish call credit spread.* VXXB is trading at 30 on August 10th. Our trader feels that there is a strong possibility that VXXB will be at or below 30 on October 19th (the third Friday of the month). He observes that the Oct 30 calls can be sold for 3.90 and the Oct 40 calls are at 1.90. He *sells* the Oct 30/40 calls for a credit of 2.00 (3.90 – 1.90). If he is correct in his assumption and VXXB closes at or below 30 on October 19th, both calls will expire worthless on October 19th and he will keep the 2.00 credit or $200 per spread contract. The maximum loss is the width of the strikes (10.00) – the credit received (2.00) = 8.00. The breakeven value of VXXB at expiration is 30.00 + 2.00 = 32.00 (the lower strike + the credit).

B. *Bearish put debit spread.* VXXB is trading at 30 on August 10th. Our trader feels that there is a strong possibility that VXXB will be at or below 30 on October 19th (the third Friday of the month). He observes that the Oct 30 puts can be sold for 4.00 and the Oct 40 puts can be purchased for 12.00. He *buys* the Oct 30/40 puts for a debit of 8.00 (12.00 – 4.00). If he is correct in his assumption and VXXB closes at 30 on October 19th, the Oct 40 puts will be worth

10.00 at expiration and the Oct 30 puts will expire worthless.[34] The profit is 10.00 − 8.00 = 2.00. The maximum loss is the amount of the debit = 8.00. The breakeven value of VXXB at expiration is 40.00 − 8.00 = 32.00 (the higher strike - the debit). These are the same maximum profit and breakeven as the bearish call credit spread.

Selling Deep-In-the-Money Puts

For several years, OptionVue sponsored monthly meetings for option traders in Chicago. I always looked forward to these meetings, which usually involved presentations by some of the best options traders at the CBOE. One successful trader offered up a simple strategy for making money. The trader would sell deep out-of-the-money puts with distant expiration dates including LEAPs (Long Term Equity Anticipation Securities). Due to market volatility at the time, he suggested entering limit sell orders 5-10% above current quotes (which for puts means when the market sells off).

Selling deep in-the-money puts does involve risks. If the value of the underlying drops more than the premium received there will be potential losses. However, the implementation of this strategy has proven to be very profitable for me and my clients on a consistent basis and works very well in an upward trending market. Warren Buffett has pointed out that the DJIA went from 66 to 11,219 during the 20th century. Add dividends to that figure and shareholders have averaged 7-8% gains annually for the past 100 years. Today (8/9/2018) the DJIA stands at 25,500. Even with major market selloffs, such as 1929, 2001-03 and 2008-09, it would be hard to argue that the long-term trend of the market is anything other than up which makes put selling an attractive long-term strategy. While there have been infrequent periods when my positions were underwater at the time of expiration, I have successfully rolled those positions forward on every occasion.

---

[34] If VXXB is trading below 30 at expiration, the profit and maximum loss is the same. E.g. if VXXB closes at 28, the following would apply: Profit = 12.00 (value of Oct 40 long put) − 2.00 (value of Oct 30 short put) − 8.00 (amount of debit) = 2.00.

I have refined and adopted this strategy for several years with great results. I like to sell in-the-money put options on my four favorite exchange traded funds, QQQ, SPY, IWM and DIA, with laddered quarterly expiration dates. I particularly look to establish new positions following periods of market retracement. I start with the nearest quarterly expiration and add further out expirations when the markets present an opportunity to do so at attractive prices. Most recently, that opportunity arose in February/March 2018 when the stock market entered a correction phase (down 10%). While the use of limit orders may mean that you miss out on an opportunity to implement a position, more times than not the market will gyrate sufficiently to hit your limit price. And if it doesn't, don't get discouraged. No one ever lost money by not implementing a trade and there will always be other opportunities like or better than the one you wanted to establish. Patience is definitely a virtue when it comes to trading. Way too many traders, especially retail or new ones, tend to force a trade when conditions are not optimal. Let the market come to you. Don't chase the market!

Once again, in order to maximize your profit potential, take advantage of the following rules:

- Do not try to time the market. However, market corrections (10% or more) have proven to be excellent entry points for this trade.

- Ladder your investments by using different maturity dates.

- Scale into your positions by adding to position size as the market moves further from your initial position. Yes, this is a form of doubling down.

- Keep the size of each individual trade small. Never "go for broke" on a single trade or broke you will soon be. No matter how enticing a particular trade, there are no sure things when it comes to trading (contrary to the title of this chapter). In the 70's and 80's, the early days of listed options, arbitragers could capture profits by purchasing a security in one market and selling the same security in another. Due to inefficiencies in pricing across different markets and exchanges, arbitrage opportunities abounded. With increased sophistication of traders using high powered computers, markets have become very efficient. Any mispricing of options or securities are extremely rare and where they do exist, they are quickly identified and picked off. Arbitrage activity results in market efficiency. There are no longer arbitrage opportunities for all but the most sophisticated traders using state-of-art technology and computer programs.

- Use limit orders to establish new option positions, especially during periods of volatile market fluctuations.

- Take defensive action when markets have moved against you. See Chapter 8.

Purchasing Discounted CDs

Several years ago, while working for Smith Barney, I had a wealthy elderly client whose primary objectives were to preserve capital and maximize the inheritance she planned to leave to her family. Sadly, she suffered from a blood disorder and had been given only a year to live. When she came to me, she had a low risk tolerance and a large fixed-income portfolio made up primarily of short-term FDIC Insured Certificates of Deposit. At the time, one-year CDs were paying around 1.5% interest. The value of fixed income instruments is inversely correlated with interest rates. As interest rates rise, the fair market value of the fixed income security declines. This effect is greater the longer the maturity of the instrument. So, if you buy a 5-year CD paying 3% interest, and the 5-year interest rate increases to 3.5%, the principal value of the CD declines proportionately. That is why bond investors consider a bond's duration when selecting which instrument to buy. Duration is a measure of a bond's sensitivity to interest rate changes. The higher the bond's duration, the greater its sensitivity to changes in interest rates. So typically, when advising elderly clients as to which bonds (or CDs) to purchase, the advisor would recommend bonds with a low duration.

By multiplying a bond's duration by the change in interest rates, the investor can estimate the percentage price change for the bond as interest rates change. For example, let's assume that bonds with a duration of 3.25 years are purchased. If prevailing interest rates subsequently increase by 50 basis points (0.50%), the approximate percentage decline in the bond's price would be -3.25 x .005 = -0.01625 or -1.625%. So, bonds purchased for $100,000 would now be worth only $98,375. As a result, risk-averse investors (especially elderly ones) generally prefer to buy bonds with a short duration.

However, what if the issuer of the bond would agree to repurchase the CD for par if the holder dies? Such a promise would largely remove concerns associated with longer durations. As it turns out, most CDs (as well as some corporates) contain a "survivor's option" commonly referred to as a "death put" provision which gives the bondholder's beneficiary the right to sell the bond back to the original issuer at full par value in the event of the bondholder's death. Consequently, if an elderly person or person in poor health purchases a 15-year CD in the secondary market which – due to a rising interest rate environment – is heavily discounted (the effect of a steep duration), the investment will likely outperform ones with a much higher level of risk. In the event that the person dies before the CD or bond matures, his or her heirs will be able to sell it back to the issuer for par. For example, a CD purchased for less than par, say at a discount of .07 (or for a price of .93) will be worth 1.0 upon the death of the holder. Or in dollar terms, a $100,000 CD purchased for $93,000 may, upon the death of the holder, be resold to the issuer for $100,000, netting a $7,000 profit plus interest payments received. In this instance, the yield-to-maturity (altered by the holder's short life expectancy) is significantly higher than other risk adjusted investments. Suppose that the purchaser died one year after purchasing such a discounted CD with a coupon of 3%. The return on investment would be as follows:

Purchase price = $93,000
Interest paid = $3,000
Redeemed at par = $100,000
Profit = $10,000 ($3,000 interest + $7,000 principal)

Thomas J. Homer, JD, CFP®

Percent Gain = 10.75%

Not a bad return on an FDIC Certificate of Deposit!

Having successfully utilized this strategy for numerous elderly clients over the years, I have been somewhat surprised that issuers have never taken steps to close this loophole by limiting the death put feature to those purchasing original issues. Until then, this strategy offers the closest thing to a high-return, low-risk trade. The strategy is particularly advantageous during rising interest rate environment as it is easier to find discounted CDs selling in the secondary markets.

CHAPTER THIRTEEN

Know Your Margin

Margin accounts allow clients to borrow funds from their broker to buy securities in their non-qualified (taxable) accounts. Typically, clients can borrow up to 50% against the value of stocks and other investment securities in their account and can use the borrowed cash for personal purposes or to make additional investments. The percentage amount varies with different investments. Most brokerage firms encourage clients to establish "margin accounts" rather than "cash accounts" because it encourages the customer to buy more securities and allows the broker to charge interest. Margin allows investors and traders to leverage their investments.

Margin accounts are not generally available for IRAs or other tax-preferenced accounts. Each brokerage firm has the right to define which investments among stocks, bonds, or mutual funds can be purchased on margin. To allow clients to use margin in their tax-qualified accounts would jeopardize the tax preference afforded to such investments.

When you establish a margin account, there are both initial and maintenance margin requirements. A brokerage firm has the right to increase the minimum amount required in a margin account, make a margin call at any time, and sell securities without notice, and even sue the client if he does not immediately satisfy the margin call. A margin call occurs when the value of the investments and cash in an account fall below the maintenance margin amount. The investor must deposit additional funds or sell a portion of the portfolio to fund the margin call. If the investor doesn't adequately fund the account following a margin call, the broker will sell some of the stocks in the account to make up the shortfall. In cash accounts the maximum loss is the totality of the client's deposits. In a margin account there is the potential for the client to lose more money than the funds deposited in his account. For these reasons, a margin account is most suitable for sophisticated investors with thorough understandings of the additional investment risks and requirements posed by margin accounts.

Even though option sellers do not actually borrow funds from their broker, sufficient capital must be maintained in order to protect against losses. Under Regulation T, the Federal Reserve Board requires all short sale accounts to have 150% of the value of the short sale at the time the sale is initiated. The 150% consists of 100% of the short sale proceeds plus an additional 50% of the value of the short sale. For example, if an investor initiates a short sale for 100 shares at $100 per share, the value of the short sale is $10,000. The initial margin requirement would be the $10,000 proceeds along with an additional $5,000, for a total of $15,000. Similar rules apply to short option positions. Brokers are allowed to impose stricter margin requirements than those required by federal regulations. Most brokers calculate on a running basis the amount of "buying power" in your account at any given time. Fortunately, in a short straddle or straddle position, the margin requirements are imposed on only one side of the transaction. Why you ask? Because it is not possible to lose on both sides of such a bet. Either the calls will expire worthless or the puts, but not both (unless at expiration, the value of the options is "pinned"[35] to the strike price of the straddle or located on the bridge of the strangle in which case you will have realized the maximum profit on the position).

---

[35] Pinning occurs when the market price of the underlying security at the time of the option's expiration is identical (or very close) to the option's strike price.

Leverage works great when you make a profitable trade. You will be happy when the increased value of the securities you purchased exceeds the rate of interest you are paying on margin. Conversely, when the value of the securities declines, such leverage can wreak havoc on your portfolio and may well take you out of your trade even when you are convinced that the market is about to rebound in your favor. Margin calls can and often do defeat the client's investment or trading strategy and lead to a strong probability of failure over time.

The greatest threat to any stock trading strategy is being overleveraged. No matter how confident you are with respect to a particular trade, there is always the possibility that you are wrong or that unforeseen events will turn the trade into a loser. The only remedy is to trade ONLY when you are adequately capitalized. Trading on a shoestring budget is recipe for disaster. Staying power is paramount to long-term successful trading.

Traders may be averse to margin requirements for large deposits of cash in their brokerage accounts to support option selling, especially since margin deposits generally do not earn interest. After all, they may reason, option writing results in premium being paid into your account and no brokerage firm funds are required to implement the trades. However, losses can result in substantial losses which must be subsidized by the trader. The margin requirements are designed to assure that ability. The good news is that most brokerage firms give margin credit for securities owned. Stock and other holdings are generally credited at 50%. For traders like me who prefer not to own stock, it makes more sense to purchase treasury securities which are generally credited at 90% for margin purposes because of low risk level associated with treasuries. Some brokers afford the same or similar level of marginability for certificates of deposit, or agency securities, such as Fannie Mae or Freddie Mac bonds. You should check with your broker for their specific policy. The ability to use such low-risk, interest-bearing securities as collateral for margin purposes, allows the trader to earn interest on the cash required for margin purposes. While higher rates of interest can usually be earned on longer maturity bonds, I prefer short-term treasury bills to avoid interest rate risk associated with bonds with longer maturities and duration and also to provide for greater liquidity in the event that the bonds need to be converted to cash.

CHAPTER FOURTEEN

Enhancing Returns – Reducing Risk

As powerful a strategy as POWER has proven to be, all investment strategies can benefit from other time-tested trading and investing techniques designed to enhance returns and reduce risk and volatility. Astute investors and experienced financial advisors use a number of strategies to accomplish these objectives. Included in these strategies are dollar-cost- averaging, laddering, scaling, and diversification.

Thomas J. Homer, JD, CFP®

DOLLAR COST AVERAGING

	Investment	Cost Per Share	No. of Shares
1ST Month	$180	$12	15
2nd Month	$180	$10	18
3rd Month	$180	$9	20
4th Month	$180	$9	20
5th Month	$180	$10	18
6th Month	$180	$12	15
Totals	$1,080		106

Average Cost per Share = $1,080/106 = $10.19

Portfolio Value at Month 6 = 106 X $12 = $1,272

Gain (Loss) = $1,272 - $1,080 = $192

Percentage Gain (Loss) = $192/$1,080 = 17.8%

Annualized Return = 17.8% X 2 = 35.6%

As discussed in Chapter 10, market timing is a sucker bet. Dollar-cost averaging is an investment technique in which a fixed dollar amount is invested in a particular fund or security at pre-determined intervals, regardless of the share price. The investor purchases more shares when prices are low and fewer shares when prices are high.

The advantage of dollar-cost-averaging is that this method of investing helps smooth out the market's ups and downs. By investing during market dips, you can significantly enhance your long-term return potential when the market rebounds. This is especially true for a stock market which has shown an upward bias since its inception.

As applied to my option writing strategy, I prefer to sell a limited number of options at intervals, rather than large bets at any one time. By using this approach, I am really engaging in dollar-cost-averaging with options.

Laddering

Laddering is a term normally associated with bond investments. A bond ladder is a strategy that attempts to minimize interest-rate risks associated with fixed-income securities while managing cash flows for the individual investor. In simpler terms, a bond ladder is the name given to a portfolio of bonds with different maturities.

Suppose you had $100,000 to invest in bonds. You do not currently contemplate that you will need to use those funds for the foreseeable future, but you don't want to tie your money up indefinitely. You could buy a bond or CD for $100,000 which matures in five years and when it comes due, reinvest the proceeds in a new five-year bond. You tell your financial advisor your plan, but she recommends instead of buying one bond, that you buy five bonds. By using the bond ladder approach, you would buy five $20,000 bonds with one, two, three, four, and five-year maturities, respectively. These bonds would each represent a different rung on the bond ladder. As soon as the shortest bond (the one-year bond) matures, you will reinvest the proceeds in a new five-year bond. In other words, you will be "climbing the ladder".

Your advisor explains that there are two main advantages to the ladder approach. First, by staggering the maturity dates, you won't be locking into an investment with a single duration. She explains that if prevailing interest rates increase, the value of bonds previously issued will decrease. No reasonable investor would be willing to pay par for your bond if she could buy a newly issued bond with a higher coupon. Therefore, you would have to discount your bond if you wished to sell it before maturity. By using a bond ladder, you smooth out the fluctuations in the market because you have a bond maturing each year. If interest rates are higher after one year, you will be able to add a new bond to your portfolio paying a higher coupon, and thereby increasing the average yield of your bonds. Laddering helps protect against interest rate risk.

The second advantage of a bond ladder is that it provides investors with steady cash flows. This flexibility is especially important to retired individuals because they may depend on the cash flows from investments as a source of income. Even for younger investors, a bond ladder allows for greater liquidity which can be very important if unexpected expenses arise.

While laddering is usually discussed in connection with the purchase of fixed-income instruments, such as bonds and CDs, the concept is equally applicable to selling options. One-third of my positions are generally established in the near expiration month, one-third in the second month, and one-third in the third month. Upon expiration of the near month, I reestablish new positions in the new third month, adjusting the strike price to reflect an at-the-money or near-the-money strike price, which is often at a strike price greater or lesser than that of the expiring option. In so doing, I am continually adjusting the overall delta of my positions with a view toward maintaining a neutral position. Some delta neutral strategists would make more frequent, perhaps daily, adjustments to maintain near-neutral positions at all time. I am not an adherent to such strict rules because (a) frequent trading results in greater execution costs, and (b) markets tend to fluctuate above and below fair value and I prefer not to chase it like dog with a stick.

Scaling

As applied to stock investing, "scaling" is the strategy of purchasing additional shares as the prices decrease. To "scale-in" means to set a target price and then invest in increments as the stock falls below that price. The concept has equal applicability to options. Of course, you will always want to establish a new position at what you believe to be a favorable price. But it is rare when you have selected the exact best price. More frequently, you enter a position only to find out that you could have obtained a more favorable price had you only waited. The problem is that tops and bottoms are elusive targets and ever-changing. Rather than suffering from buyer's remorse when the price moves away from your position (and you experience losses in your position – never fun), you should look upon it as an opportunity to convert your position to one with a more favorable cost basis.

No matter how attractive you believe an investment to be, I strongly recommend that you start out with a small position and gradually add to it as prices become more attractive. This is called scaling in to a position. One of the biggest mistakes traders make is to put too much investment capital into a single investment. Very often "a good investment opportunity" would have become an even better investment opportunity had you only waited. By making small incremental bets, you have capital remaining to put to work when conditions become even more favorable. Scaling is really a way of dollar-cost-averaging so that when the market turns in your favor, your profits on your small bets will be greater than had you made a single big bet.

I once read a book on gambling which advocated double-down betting as a sure way of winning. The idea was to place a minimum bet, say $5, on a game of chance like craps on the pass line (or on the don't pass line if you prefer, but be prepared for dirty looks from your fellow gamblers especially the shooter). If you lose the first bet, make a second bet of $10. If you lose again, place a $20 bet and so on. Eventually, as the theory goes, you will eventually win recapturing all of your losses plus a $5 profit. The problem with this strategy is that most casinos have table limits, or your resources are limited, either of which could well send you back to the drawing board, or more likely, into the nearest bar. The key to making all strategies work long-term is sustainability.

Diversification

I use ETFs rather than individual equities as the underlying in order to achieve a measure of diversification. I am not a stock picker and have never pretended to be. SPYs are composed of baskets of stocks mirroring the S&P 500 stocks, QQQ's the Nasdaq 100 (which by the way is not the same as the NASDAQ), IWMs which consist of Russell 2000 (or small cap) stocks and occasionally Diamonds (DIA). While these four ETFs are correlated, there have certainly been times when one outperforms or lags the other for a period of time. The important thing is that if an individual equity that is part of the index blows up, the other components help keep the valuation of the ETF from imploding.

By investing in ETFs as opposed to individual stocks, you can minimize "stock risk". Investing in only one or even a handful of stocks is risky because the investor's portfolio is adversely affected when one of those stocks declines in price. Mutual funds and ETFs mitigate stock risk by investing in a large number of stocks. In that way, when the value of a single stock drops, it has a smaller effect on the value of the diversified portfolio. It is the prevailing view that a minimum of 20 different stocks is necessary to minimize stock risk. Moreover, holding positions in different ETFs, such as QQQ's, SYPs, IWMs, and DIAs at the same time mitigates against market sector risk.

By eliminating individual stock risk and minimizing market sector risks, we can allow our option writing strategy to take advantage of time-decay, which leads to consistent profitable trading.

CHAPTER FIFTEEN

End Game

There is more than one way to make money in the stock market, and more ways to lose it. POWER is designed to profit from investor greed and fear. POWER capitalizes on the inverse correlation between the price of put and call options. Coupled with time decay, POWER can provide the winning edge enjoyed by casino operators and insurance companies. When further enhanced by the time-tested principles of diversification, laddering, scaling, and dollar-cost-averaging, POWER can lead to extraordinary profits well in excess of the S&P 500 index and with less market risk.

Like casinos, POWER allows you to profit from the greed of speculators and from thrill seekers. And like insurance companies, POWER allows you to capitalize on investor fear and the willingness of hedgers to overpay for protection.

At the same time, investors and traders seeking a higher rate of return than that provided by low or no-risk investments, such as treasuries and CDs, must be willing to accept some level of risk to achieve more lofty objectives. Although the POWER strategy consistently outperforms the S&P 500 and other stock indices, it is not without risk. During periods of market upheaval, there will be unavoidable periods of stress and drawdowns. However, patience and faith will generally be rewarded, while panic and impatience are usually punished.

Just prior to the completion of this book (early 2019) the stock market is recovering from a year-end market temporary meltdown. The S&P 500 declined 14% in the final quarter of 2018, dropping 9.2% in December, the worst month of December since the Great Depression. The Dow fell 653 points on Christmas Eve alone after dropping over 1000 points intraday, in Scrooge-like fashion. While the POWER strategy is not immune from market volatility, the late 2018 losses were significantly offset by expiring short calls which generated maximum profits on those positions. As a result, my pain was substantially less than that experienced by investors holding unprotected long positions. And even better, within a few short weeks my portfolio has largely recovered from the December drawdowns. I fully expect to achieve new highs this year. While it is not always possible to enjoy positive returns during turbulent markets, POWER has generated exceptional returns over time and achieves an alpha that would be the envy of most money managers.

During normal periods, the POWER strategy has significantly outperformed the S&P 500 Index often by 700 – 800 basis points (7% to 8%) and occasionally even more. Over time, that type of outperformance has provided my family with the supplemental income needed to pay for college tuition, vacations, and other needs while allowing me to pursue my chosen professional endeavors.

Moreover, it is important to remember that relative success is achieved by outperforming the market rather than by absolute returns. A 5% loss when the S&P 500 index declines 10% adds more value to your portfolio than a gain of 15% when the S&P 500 index is up by the same amount. No strategy, including POWER, returns profits during every market cycle. However, POWER is designed to outperform the S&P 500 during sideway markets, down markets as well as during up-trending markets. While the strategy underperforms the index during raging bull markets, POWER has proven over time to be a winning strategy when implemented with discipline and techniques described in this book.

Some readers may question the appropriateness of the word "passive" in POWER. After all, the ongoing requirement to establish new positions and take defensive actions outlined in this book may at first blush appear to require considerable proactive participation. While the POWER portfolio does require monitoring and adjustments especially when stock market volatility has caused its combined delta to stray too far from its initial neutral position (+/- 0.75), the instances of such occurrences are infrequent. During periods of normal market activity, the portfolio requires little effort to implement. Remember, time is your ally. The passage of time works in your favor.

I would, however, urge those new to option trading to start out slowly. Building a healthy portfolio takes time. Don't become impatient and shoot for the moon. As the saying goes, "pigs get fat, hogs get slaughtered!" The most common reason for investor and trader failure is undercapitalization and margin calls. If you are overleveraged, it is only a matter of time before that leverage will work against you and force you out of positions involuntarily. You must be properly capitalized and understand your broker's margin requirements. The second most common reason for failure is the tendency of overly aggressive investors to wager too much on any one trade. No matter how attractive a trade may appear at the time, markets are highly unpredictable. There is no sure thing when it comes to trading. For each trade you make, there is someone who has taken the opposite side. Most importantly, it is imperative that you risk only those discretionary funds that are not needed for current living expenses.

I was motivated to write this book by the success that I have enjoyed over many years of selling options. The methods described in this book have evolved over time, initially as theories and then tested by real-time market trading. There have been setbacks and disappointments along the way. My personal experiences have shaped the lessons presented in this book. It is my hope that you will find the POWER strategy as profitable as I have over a long and rewarding trading career. If so, this project will have been well worth the endeavor. Good luck and good trading!

Tom Homer, 2019

www.ingramcontent.com/pod-product-compliance
Lightning Source LLC
Chambersburg PA
CBHW030848180526
45163CB00004B/1492